M.

M

The Racing Edge

The Racing Edge

by Ted Turner and Gary Jobson

Illustrations by Bill King

A Rutledge Book
Simon and Schuster
New York

Prepared and produced by Rutledge Books, Inc.
Published by SIMON and SCHUSTER
A Division of Gulf & Western Corporation
Simon & Schuster Building
Rockefeller Center
1230 Avenue of the Americas
New York, New York 10020
Manufactured in the United States of America
First Edition

Library of Congress in Publication Data
Turner, Ted.
    The racing edge.

    "A Rutledge book."
    Includes index.
    1. Yacht racing.   2. Sailing I. Jobson, Gary,
joint author. II. Title.
GV826.5.T8   797.1'4   78-22042
ISBN 0-671-24419-1

For: Bill, Bunky, Conn, Dick, L. J., Marty,
Paul, Richie, Robbie, and Stretch

Pages 2-3: *Ted Turner at the helm of* Tenacious *as it duels* Running Tide *(4444) in the Annapolis Yacht Club Fall Series*. Pages 4-5: Courageous *(left) and* Independence *speed testing off Boston.*

Contents

Foreword

The winning sailor consistently does everything just a little bit better than the competition. He anticipates wind shifts more accurately than the rest of the fleet, plays his sails with more finesse, handles his boat more effectively, knows his competition better, and has a sounder practice routine. His racing edge is a composite advantage, built from all the different phases of sailboat racing. This is a book for the sailor with the interest and patience to build that racing edge for himself.

For close to a year we prepared for the 1977 America's Cup defense, trying to come as close as possible to perfecting the art of sailboat racing. We believe we made some real breakthroughs. And much of what we discovered and employed in that campaign applies to sailboat racing in boats of all sizes. We discovered the greater efficiency of sailing by air speed rather than boat speed. We practiced the tactical uses of the hand-bearing compass. We honed new starting and practicing methods, plus boat-handling techniques. In this volume we have tried to record systematically everything about sailboat racing that has worked for us, in big boats and small. Some of it is standard, but much is new, from attitudes to techniques.

Winning sailboat races is neither magical nor mechanical. There are no shortcuts. It takes thoroughly practiced skills and a thoroughly practical philosophy. Here we would like to present you with both. We hope you will come away from this book with many new tips and a better understanding of racing in general, including just the simple fun of it. *The Racing Edge* may not make you a champion sailor, but we believe it shows you what you need to become one. The rest is up to you.

Ted Turner and Gary Jobson

Part 1

Turner and Jobson: In Conversation

the tactician interviews the skipper

I hear you talking to reporters a lot about why we compete in sailing and other sports. What do you think is the value of competition, particularly in sailing?

I would just say that we have a need to compete. It's as natural as sleeping or eating. We have a need to excel. And sailing is very good at bringing it out.

What challenges you to win? Of all the people I've ever sailed with, I've never seen anybody as strong-willed to win on the racecourse. What is that?

I've got a larger dose of motivation than most people have. Some people are born fleet of foot, make great runners. When basic characteristics were doled out, I got more than my share of competitiveness. That's probably all. In fact, it may not be all that healthy.

Some people say that competition can bring out the worst in people, and others that competition can bring out the best.

I would say there are a lot of people who get more enjoyment and camaraderie and friendship out of sailing competitively than in sailing just for relaxation. But the competition ought to be kept in perspective. Sailing is sport—at least, it's supposed to be. It ought to be fun. That doesn't mean you can't give it everything you have; but when poor sportsmanship and skinning the edges of the rules and so forth fall into it, as they have in certain areas, that's not good. Sailboat racing ought to be fun.

Do you think the key to success in sailing is persistence—just plugging away at it? Some people sail for forty years and never get in the top half of the fleet.

I'd say that's one of the qualities you have to have to win in anything. You have to be persistent and you have to be dedicated. You have to be hardworking. I've never run into the guy who could win at the top level in anything today and didn't have the right attitude, didn't give it everything he had, at least while he was doing it; wasn't prepared and didn't have the whole program worked out. On the other hand, you have to have the ability and you've got to have good sense. And that's true in every aspect of life. Sailing is a brains game to a large degree, as well as physical. And you've got to be able to figure out what's going wrong and correct it. To get to the top, you have to have the ability and the attitude, I'd say.

Do you think physical conditioning plays an important part in it?

Certainly in certain areas of sailing it does. In sailing a boat like the Shields the skipper could be a one-legged man and do all right. But when you're sailing something like a Flying Dutchman or a Finn or a 470, any of the high-performance boats, certainly you have to be in tremendous physical shape—quick and agile. Also when you're sailing on a large boat such as a twelve-meter, you have to have quick hands. And you have to be strong, maybe up to a football or basketball level of physical conditioning. If you're navigating, the biggest physical strain is the cranking of a backstay, although on *Courageous* that was no small job either.

Where do you think you can find the best competition in sailing?

It's all over the place. Take Atlanta, for instance. Sailing up on the lakes in Atlanta, you normally have light air, pretty shifty, and some of the sailors who sail up there, primarily every weekend, could blow the brains off a lot of the great guys, say from Buzzards Bay or San Francisco. It's always difficult to go into any club, whether it's Barnegat Bay or wherever, and go against the locals, since they know the tidal conditions and everything. So I'd say that the competition is good and interesting just about everywhere in the country.

Who would you say are some of the great yachtsmen of the day?

You're talking about big-boat sailors? Small-boat sailors? There are just so many. You know, a lot of sailors don't get the recognition that you do sailing big boats because I guess the newspapers and magazines like to write about the bigger boats. Well, elephants get a lot more attention than the ants do.

There are a lot of guys sailing small boats who never leave their own classes but would be excellent on the big-boat circuit if they had the desire or the money or the opportunity to get into it. So I really think it's hard to choose, though some obviously come to mind right away: Paul Elvstrom and Buddy Melges; those two would be a couple of the absolute greatest. There are lots of other ones—Peter Commette and John Bertrand—younger guys. And you have older ones, like Bus Mosbacher. There would be literally hundreds of them, if you researched it, and most of the young guys I don't even know.

There are a lot of fellows around who take a lot from the sport, but not that many who are returning a lot. Who are some of the people who seem to balance between the two?

Anyone who has been active in helping out on the regional level and at the national level. I really believe that the USYRU [United States Yacht Racing Union] and USISA [United States International Sailing Association] have a lot of fine people who have helped out, in the Olympic effort and so forth. And once again, the list of people without whose work sailing couldn't take place is really endless. It includes committee people at every level, class presidents and officers, local commodores at yacht-racing associations, vice-commodores of the local yacht clubs. . . .

What are the great offshore races in the world? Which would you rank as, say, the top five or six?

I prefer courses that keep the fleet fairly close together, so that fluky weather conditions are minimized. A point-to-point race over a wide expanse of ocean—the Bermuda or Honolulu race, for example—can be a challenge, but it is not as true a test of sailing ability as the St. Petersburg–Fort Lauderdale race, say, or even the Miami–Nassau race, in which you have two marks that you have to turn. That keeps the fleet pretty much on the same course. I would say that the Fasnet Race is probably the most competitive one in the world.

How about the Mackinacs?

They're great too. All the big-name races are great, because they attract top-level competition. I like the Hobart Race, too, because the coasts of Australia and Tasmania keep the fleet fairly close together.

This may be a good time to say that I enjoy fleet racing actually more than match racing. It's always really interesting when the boats are closely matched and the crews and skippers are evenly matched in ability. But match racing just isn't as challenging, on the average, as racing against a twenty- or thirty-boat fleet. If you're a little faster than the other guy, it's no contest. In a fleet race, a guy that's a little bit slower, for whatever reason, does have an outside chance. In a match race, he really doesn't since he's always being covered.

What was the roughest race you've been on?

Obviously, the Chicago–Mackinac, which you just mentioned, would be a candidate. It can be nasty and cold on the lakes, even in summer. The Sydney–Hobart race, with those southerly busters coming up from the South Pole, that's really rough, and the Trans-Atlantic race, with the westerly gales, can be pretty bad, even though the wind is

Ondine *recovering from a broach in a fifty-knot gust.*

primarily behind you. The Lauderdale race is another one, if a norther comes through in the winter—or any SORC [Southern Ocean Racing Conference] race when a real bad cold front comes through, which is fairly often.

I haven't been with you when it's really rough—blowing sixty—but I've been with you at the point where safety becomes a factor. You want to hold the chute as long as you can, but then it starts blowing just too hard for the chute, so you take it down a little early. Where do you draw the line?

Fortunately, I always have pretty strong boats. I have not allowed myself to get caught up in the craze for light boats and equipment. When the wind starts to really come on, it's better to be prepared than to have to go right to the edge. In other words, once you've gotten down to your storm canvas, you may not be going very fast, but there's not much that can go wrong. You're not likely to lose your rig if you've got a good stick in the boat. Incidentally, we discovered in the Sydney–Hobart race on the *Pied Piper* that a great storm rig, fast as the devil for downwind running in extremely heavy air and heavy seas, is a mainsail—a number two genoa— winged out to windward and a reacher out to leeward. That's a heck of a good rig if you have a double-grooved headstay, as most boats do now. The boat was much more controllable than it was with a spinnaker, and we were going, I think, just as fast, maybe faster, because we weren't yawing or rolling as much.

The most frightening time for me, and I think when you get into the most trouble, is when you have a spinnaker up going downwind in marginal conditions. The wind is strong, and the seas are running pretty rough. You never know when you're going to wipe out. Upwind it's not that bad, be-

cause no matter how hard it blows all you have to do is put on smaller sails. It's uncomfortable changing them, but once you are down to the right canvas, the reaching is not a problem—up to fifty or sixty knots, I think.

When you're going downwind in that kind of breeze, do you ever sail by-the-lee?

By-the-lee in heavy wind is pretty dangerous. And in the kind of winds we're talking about, you can't fly a blooper because the bloopers are basically light and they'll blow out. Your blooper usually blows out just about the time you really need it.

Let's face it, though: only two or three percent of sailboat racing is done in winds over thirty to thirty-five knots. You're not going to win much by being a great sailor in winds over thirty knots.

When do you set aside the pushing hard and racing hard and start thinking about safety? When the crew can no longer handle it, or when you're afraid the boat's not going to be able to handle it, or a combination of both?

The roughest conditions I've encountered were during winter cruises when we were shorthanded, when I first started ocean racing. I used to go out with crews that were not experienced, and you get in a lot of trouble there, but over the last ten years we've always had a large-enough and competent-enough crew, so I've never had to worry much about the safety of the crew. We take all the precautions on that. For instance, the guys we haul aloft are normally extremely competent and experienced. They have enough sense to know when they can go up, but if I thought it was really dangerous, I'd just get by without replacing a halyard. I have to say, I've never been out in the kind of breaking seas— eighty- or a-hundred-knot weather—that Adlard Coles writes about. That might be something you encounter once every twenty-five years or something. I've been racing for thirty years, and I've never been out in eighty-knot winds, except in small-boat racing when a line squall would come—you know, sort of Bam! and over you'd go.

Do you remember when the seventy-knot line squall came through right after one of the America's Cup trial races?

Yeah, but we had the sails down—

We were towing.

The committee called that off—wisely, or it would have had two twelve-meters towed in without their spars. The spars probably would have been blown over, with the sails blown out completely or else flogged to ribbons.

When was the first time you aspired to win the America's Cup? Is it something you always wanted to do?

I think the first time was when I was in college at Brown. I had the good fortune to watch the first twelve-meter defense, in 1958, and I remember the boats: *Columbia* and *Sceptre*. I was out there watching the first race. We were on a sailboat about thirty feet long, owned by the family of a friend of mine. We were near Castle Hill, and they towed the boats by·—both white, if I remember. The crews were all big, muscular men, with their matching shirts on. I'm sure that at the time I didn't just decide I was going to go out and win the Cup, but I was pretty impressed. At the time I had never sailed on anything bigger than a Y Flyer or a Lightning.

I remember when I thought Lightnings were like J-boats. I was ten years old and I was sailing a Penguin. I thought, Boy, if I ever get a Lightning, that would really be out of sight! And then when I did, I really enjoyed it. Lightnings are a lot of fun.

In fact, I enjoyed every boat I ever sailed. It doesn't really matter what size

Turner winning the Demitasse Cup in Newport, sailing a Dyer-Dhow.

Jobson at the helm of Tenacious, *Turner standing amidships, off Annapolis.*

boat you're sailing. The sport is the same, whether it's a Penguin or an Interclub dinghy or a Laser or a twelve-meter or a Class A offshore racer. Same wind, same waves, same principles; just a lot less agony and grief in a smaller boat.

Some people think that the best big-boat sailors are the ones who have gone through the fire in small boats first.

Absolutely. I say that a good small-boat background is essential, starting with dinghies and then on to a little sloop, with spinnaker and so forth. I mean, to go straight into big boats without sailing small boats at least a number of years would be like trying to go to college without having gone to high school.

Do you think it's good to stay in touch with small boats when sailing big ones?

It's good if you have the time to do it. If you ask me, sailing is so much fun that it's best to do it in all sizes of boats. The average weekend sailor might be able to make a couple of big-boat races a year or something like that. The rest of the time he's sailing in his own club on small boats. Of course, most people sail small boats and don't really get a chance to race offshore, because of the time and money involved.

A couple of years ago, before I bought the baseball team, I got a Y Flyer again, and I had as much fun sailing that as I do the bigger boats. The only reason I'm not sailing every weekend in small boats right now is simply because I don't have the time. But they're just as much fun as the big boats, maybe more.

The main thing is to buy a boat you can afford to campaign in a first-class manner. There's nothing sadder than to see a guy with a boat for which he can't afford first-class equipment because the boat's too large. It's like buying a bigger house than you can afford to maintain. If you want a big boat, the thing to do is check out a used one, particularly in one-design. Normally all it will need is sails and maybe a few more fittings and so forth. You just have to be sure to weigh it to make sure it's not too heavy.

One thing, though. Whatever size boat, it's important to race a high-performance boat if you want to raise your level of racing. Low-performance boats teach tactics, since they are relatively close in speed; high-performance boats teach good boat-handling techniques, and that is how to improve most quickly. If you want to be really good, you need to be in a high-performance or Olympic-class boat.

I have tended to sail the highest-performance type of boat I could, and I think it's been a major factor in my success as a sailor. I started in a Penguin, which was good experience because it requires good balance or you capsize. After several years I got into the Y Flyer, another relatively high-performance boat. And I really started making progress when I got into the Flying Dutchman, which in the sixties was probably the hottest boat around. My keelboat sailing began in a 5.5-meter, which was definitely the most sophisticated small keelboat ever built.

These days 470s are excellent. So are Lasers and Finns. And there are a number of other boats in the high-performance class: the Thistle, 505, and Scows.

Ted, there really isn't that much match racing going on in this country, or in fact the world. Is this what makes the America's Cup so interesting?

Well, the biggest challenge of the America's Cup is to get *into* the America's Cup—figuring out how to get a berth. But of course the fact that the boats are so large and expensive is the reason it gets the publicity. And it does attract the best sailors.

You know, the level of racing in the America's Cup has improved. So much time and money is devoted to it that you can reach a level of performance, with the practice and continual working on the sails, that is pretty impressive. You have sailmakers sailing on the boats and working on the sails daily.

Still, I would say that going to the Olympics and winning a gold medal is a far greater challenge than defending the America's Cup, because, first of all, there's a lot more people you're competing against. There was a total of, I think, only seven boats in the entire America's Cup, whereas in the Finn class at the Olympics there are probably five to six hundred sailors who try for a slot, and those are the finest sailors. Then too, the Olympic sailor is a much younger fellow, because of the physical demands of boats like 470s, for example. It's just not a boat that somebody in his forties would be sailing. On the other hand, you're going to have a basically older group in the America's Cup anyway, because of the complexity and the money and experience required. . . .

The average age on Courageous *was thirty-three, and that was young compared with a lot of the twelve-meter campaigns of the past.*

I think we had the youngest afterguard in history. . . .

How do you put your crews together? What do you look for; what are the qualities for a successful crew?

Of course the nature of the crew depends on the size of the boat. As the boat gets bigger, you have more of a division of labor. An FD crewman, for example, has to be as skillful a sailor as there is. He's got to be the spinnaker man, the jib man, the hiking man, the tactician, the navigator. The helmsman just hangs on and tries to keep the boat going fast through the waves.

Of course, on a Laser or Finn, you are the crew. When I sailed a Finn and wasn't doing well, everybody used to say I cussed my crew. I'd talk to myself: "You stupid son-of-a-gun, you. You can hike out harder." You know— when they're going by on both sides. I found I really enjoyed sailing on two- and three-man boats more because I like the camaraderie of having somebody along.

Now, when you get on a bigger boat, the crew becomes more of an organizational deal. On a twelve-meter, you have one guy who is the tactician, one guy who is bowman, and so on down the line, with eight guys leaning over the side and a guy trimming the jib. In a way, it becomes simpler. On a twelve you can take somebody who really doesn't know that much about tactics but is a good, strong, willing worker, and he can be a very important addition to the crew just by grinding. On a big boat you also need to consider getting a group of guys who will get along with one another, especially if you're going to stay together for more than one series. Your greatest premium, though, is on organization and recruiting, just like it is in basketball and baseball. Having the experience to know what kind of equipment to get and who to put your money on.

Another thing on that. From the skipper's standpoint, and even from every crew member's, you have to be extremely tolerant when you are on an offshore boat, because people are going to make mistakes, and the more people the more mistakes. The chance for mistakes is about equal to the number of the crew squared, so every additional crew member increases that percentage quite a bit. I personally enjoy the camaraderie and the challenge of the larger group, but there are a lot of people who don't want to bother with that. I know some tremendous sailors who are not really good on large boats—not because they don't have the ability to sail them, but just because they find it difficult getting along with all those people. They can't put up with the hollering when somebody makes a mistake; they simply like to do things independently. This is one of the great things about sailing: there's room for all kinds of people.

About three hundred people have asked me, "How do you get on a twelve-meter crew?"

One way is to buy your way on. But you've got to be good then. I'd say to sail on a twelve-meter you need to be a good small-boat sailor—not necessarily a skipper, but you need to have both small-boat experience, and a lot of it, and the big-boat experience too. Most basic of all, it's good to find out who has twelve-meter aspirations, from both a syndicate and a skippering standpoint, and to get to know those people, since they pick the crew.

What were some of the qualities that helped Courageous *to win in '77?*

It's like any successful operation. It was very soundly structured and planned from the bottom up. But I would say from an overall planning and preparation standpoint, our two competitors were ahead of us. Even though our planning was excellent, theirs was certainly more lavish. In other words, they both had decided that a newer design would be faster—which is always a gamble, but usually a sound one. Normally, there is some progress in yacht design, so normally, the best new twelve-meter is a little better than the old one.

But *Courageous* was all we could get. We couldn't have gotten a new boat unless, of course, I'd wanted to sell everything I had and put it all into a twelve-meter, which I didn't do. Even as it was, I had to put up

an awful lot of money to get *Courageous* because of the financial difficulties we had in campaigning the two boats [*Mariner* and *Valiant*], which is always more difficult than just campaigning one, and also because of the poor showing that we had on *Mariner.* [Turner was replaced as the skipper of *Mariner* in 1974.] Normally, when you get clobbered as badly as we did on *Mariner,* then draw a slow twelve-meter like *Valiant,* it can't help hurting your chances quite a bit of getting another shot at it. But it turned out okay after all. I gambled that *Courageous* would be competitive, and she has turned out to be that and more. However, I don't think the basic hull was significantly faster than *Independence* or *Enterprise.*

Then, after getting the boat, I did the best I could at putting together the most mature and experienced crew I possibly could. Since the other two boats were already under way and they had already begun to select their crews before I even had a boat, they had the first- and second-round drafts and we drafted third. But there were still quite a few good guys available in the third draft. We had a couple of rookies, but also plenty of experience.

In your case, Gary, I knew you'd be super if you had a chance to get to know what I expected of you and we had a chance to get on the same wavelength. Sailing the circuit together on *Tenacious,* which wasn't a twelve-meter but was about the same size and speed, we almost had match-racing experience, particularly in the good racing we had against *Running Tide.* That was hours and hours of just sailing along and working on trying to catch or pass them or stay ahead of them, and it was very, very close. Then the Congressional Cup, with nine tough match races.

Much of the rest of the crew, as you'll

Turner sailing Cal 40 (7124) against Noel Robins in 1978 Congressional Cup. Robins skippered America's Cup challenger Australia.

recall, had sailed with me on *Mariner* and *Valiant* before, so they knew what was expected and what it was going to take to win. It helped also that we gave everyone jobs to do early on, so they could perfect their areas, and I think everyone did perfect his area. As problems arose with our sails and so forth, we sat down, and luckily we had brilliant people—brilliant, dedicated people—in every area, who had, I think, more responsibility, certainly, than Ted Hood tended to give his group. Hood kept rotating people around, and I don't think they achieved anything like the level of performance on *Independence* that we did, though had the boat been faster they might have. They seemed to have guys doing the same jobs pretty much, but they did have some problems. I remember they fired some people early on.

Above: Courageous *crew. Top row, left to right: Jobson, John Edgcomb, Paul Fuchs; bottom row: Richie Boyd, Bunky Helfrich, Turner, Marty O'Meara, Bill Jorch, Stretch Ryder, Dick Sadler, Conn Finlay. Missing: Robbie Doyle.* Right: *work during pre-start maneuver.* Overleaf: *Jobson adjusting trim tab, Jorch making calculation on computer, Doyle trimming main, and Boyd (bottom) playing genoa. Note tacking lines.*

When we got to Newport, if I remember, we had some sickness, and we brought in a couple of tremendous substitutes. You've got to have a good bench to win in anything. But other than that, I don't think we changed the crew from the first day of the summer until the last day, though of course we had tryouts for a couple of positions up in Marblehead before coming down.

I'd say we put in eight or nine hours a day every day in practice, and we were deadly serious about what we were doing, but what with the length of the campaign, I tried to keep it as light as possible, so we didn't burn ourselves out. We had plenty of energy left—emotional energy as well as physical—for a good push at the end.

I remember once in the middle of everything just taking a sail and having lunch at Block Island.

That day *Independence* broke down. Ordinarily, I don't find it beneficial just to go out and sail by yourself. It's like playing tennis by yourself; you can knock a ball up against the wall and get a little exercise doing it, but it's a pretty low-key workout. But we'd been working extremely hard, so at that point we just cruised over to Block Island. We did some tacking and jibing drills on the way over. I think we changed sails at the time just to practice, but we went the straight line. A lot of guys had never been to Block Island, and we went ashore, had lunch for an hour, then sailed back.

What about your own frame of mind, as skipper? How would you assess your emotions at the time of the America's Cup, aside from just being up for the competition?

I was ready. With all the big-boat experience that I had had in messing around with *American Eagle* and doing a lot of sailing in larger boats, one-tonners and larger, I learned plenty. You know—sailing *American Eagle* ten thousand miles and then the disastrous *Mariner* campaign, when we learned how to eat humble pie. But that in itself is something you need to learn, because in twelve-meter racing you need to have a lot of humility. You're not sailing your own boat; you're working for a committee, the New York Yacht Club selection committee, and you're working for your syndicate. So you have to be a little bit of a politician, in the better sense of the word. You have to be a gentleman, and you have to do what is expected of you on the water as well as off. I mean, going around and writing "turkey" with a grease pencil on another guy's boat, like they do in the Finn class, doesn't make sense in a twelve. If they found out who did it, you'd be taking a walk down the dock the next day. You ought to be a gentleman and make the yacht club and your competitors happy to have known you. Good sportsmanship and reasonable standards of conduct are important.

What did defending the Cup mean to you in the end, after it was all over?

Like any international-championship regatta, particularly the first time, it's a tremendous experience. I remember when I first went to the Lightning Internationals up in Buffalo. I was so impressed just to be there and meet all the real big cheeses in it. So there was excitement and elation and satisfaction at having accomplished what we set out to do, and reaching what is certainly one of the great pinnacles in yacht racing.

And there was a sense of relief, too, that it was over. I spent all year getting ready for those Cup races. When we went to Newport and when we were up there sailing, I wiped almost everything out of my mind, just about every waking moment, except for maybe a couple of hours in the evening when I'd relax and watch a ball game.

It kept building up day after day. . . .

The pressure was intense for the sum-

Hiking on trapeze during America's Cup interlude.
(The use of trapezes was illegal during the competition.)
Courageous *kept five men in hiking straps.*

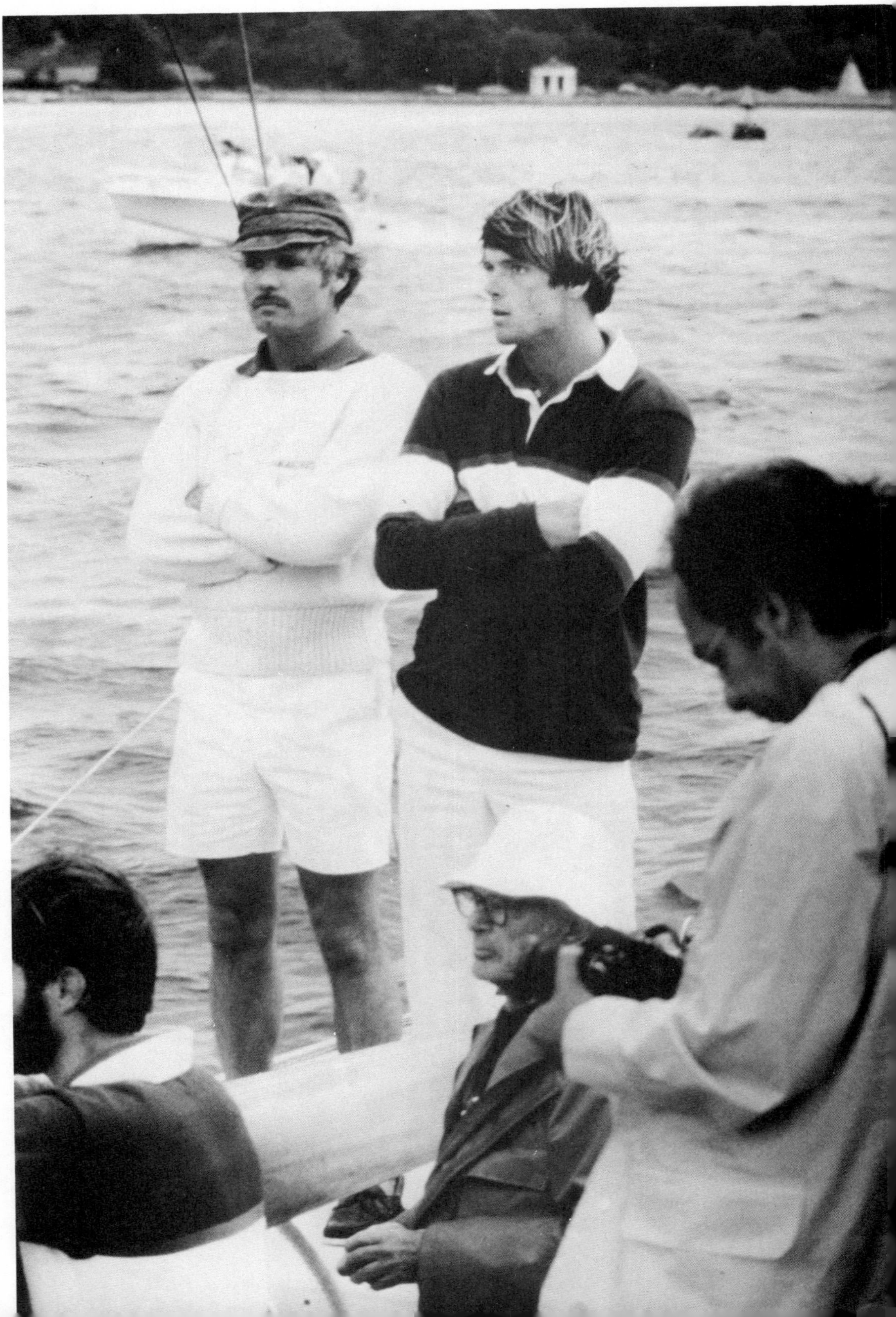

Turner and Jobson made a close and effective team, somewhat to the surprise of many observers, who expected the assertive skipper to overwhelm the young tactician. Opposite: pre-race tension; above: a victory embrace. Left: Morning strolls provided consultation time.

mer. Everyone was trying so hard to do a
perfect job, so there was a sense of relief
that it was over and we could all go home
to our regular careers, which seemed like
they would almost be vacations. I know that
every man in the crew, including myself,
felt the strain. Those races last so long.
When you're behind, you keep trying to
tack to get away, for hours and hours, and
it's so hard to do that it feels like somebody
has taken a whip and beaten you on the
back.

And there was a lot of work even when
we weren't racing or practicing. We'd watch
Ted Hood when he was sailing against *Enterprise*—we watched both Hood and North
to see how they were reacting when they
raced against each other. We checked their
sails and how they were tacking, looking for
the good things they were doing and for the
chinks in their armor. . . .

*I think knowing your competition is a very
important thing.*

It's certainly important in the America's
Cup, or any match race. A lot of it is psychological. I think our good start in June
gave us a leg up and gave our crew a sense
of elation and optimism, whereas a sense
of gloom and defeatism crept into the other
two boats. It was important that we main-
tained this edge, though we came close to
losing it in July.

Somebody said to me after it was over,
"You guys were so good. Did you ever
make mistakes?" So I told him about the
first time against *Independence* when we
were up there with all of our people green
and went into that tacking duel. Those kids
cleaned our clocks. Losing track of where
the trim tab was was kind of fun.

*That was my fault. I locked the rudder one
way and the trim tab the other.*

We just stopped—had to take two tacks
right at the mark.

Solings at Kiel Week race approaching windward mark.
With mark well to the right (out of picture), some boats clearly
have overshot it. To avoid this problem, it is advisable to
stay within the lay lines when approaching a mark.

33

Everything is great when you're winning, but when you lose and come back, that's the toughest thing. What's the secret there? We lost five in a row to Enterprise, *yet we came back to beat them.*

In my mind, we were losing in July primarily because we just had not gotten our light-air mainsail. We were using a mainsail that was a cut-down sail from *Independence.* It was a fine sail in a breeze, but it was not up to it in light air—a little short on the foot, and it had a relatively small roach. The other boats had high-roach mains. When we finally got our high-roach main, we were never defeated. Another thing. The amount of tacking we did in June and early July broke down the jibs. Those sails have only so many races in them, and all that tacking shortens the life of the sail to probably half of what it would be on an ocean race. When we got new sails, we won that big last race against *Enterprise.*

So I think the main reason for our defeat in July was sails—the fact that our sails were just worn out. Now, I think it's important to say here again how close the boats were. I mean, when we would swap jibs with *Independence,* they would beat us with a good jib. And we would beat them when the sails were changed the other way. It was that close; it was so close because the basic boat speed of all three boats through the water was just about even. This is why we have to give so much of the credit for our victory to Robbie Doyle, for recutting the sails, and also to L. J. Edgcomb and Stretch Ryder, who helped him. Having new sails was one thing, but the shape that Robbie built into them made a big difference. He was constantly recutting all our sails. And I think it was the consensus of experienced men on the selection committee, who were close to the racing, that our sails were superior.

Would you say our ability to change jibs quickly was one of our major keys to success on Courageous?

Absolutely. We had the right jibs and we had the right system and the right personnel to change them. You have to have all three. And then we had spent the time to know which ones to use under which circumstances. The right sails, the right people, the right system, and the experience to know which one should be up when. I think that particularly helped us against *Enterprise,* because I think *Independence* certainly had the right sails and knew which ones to have up. They didn't change as often as we did, but they had the system. I think maybe they didn't have as much confidence in their personnel as we did to make the changes in critical situations. And if you'll remember, Robbie Doyle, God bless his soul, didn't have as much confidence in our ability to do it as we did. But we never had a major foul-up, to my knowledge, changing a jib. We changed them a lot. We practiced it a lot, too. We practiced it because there's no room for error changing jibs on a seventy-foot boat while tacking.

As far as practicing, you had everybody following the same routine, a set routine, even on nonrace days.

It's just like in baseball: you're so much better off with a set lineup than you are changing things around, because you just can't get too proficient in what you're doing—particularly on a large boat, but even on a small one. And the more people involved, the more you have to integrate. Any one person failing to do his job in a tack or a jibe causes the jibe or tack to miscarry. Had a sail change been wrong, we could have ended up with a sail in the water, and it would have cost us the race. Just the slightest little fitting going—remember when we lost the backstay?—that's the end of the race. Your crew has to have every single, possible maneuver or circumstance, fore and aft, down to where you don't even think about what it is when it occurs, because usually when something busts or breaks or miscarries, you don't have time. You've got to have it all planned out. And you practice so that after a while nobody even has to say anything.

How do you integrate new crew? We got a new crew—two or three guys—and then you had everybody stand in their positions and sort of run through the deck for the different things, plus a disaster drill.

I try to take the experienced, qualified guys, who have sailed on the boat before, and put them in all the key positions. In offshore racing you usually just go reaching off for hours at a time, and you have plenty of time to talk things over and straighten things out. But when you go around the buoys, as we did at Newport in the du Pont series, you have no margin for error. We had a very competent crew, and except for a couple, everyone in it had practiced on the boat before. We got around the course, but not without a few fire drills, considering that it was blowing twenty to thirty the whole time.

What do you think of the trend in offshore racing toward one-design sailing—the J-24, the New York 40s, Aphrodite 101?

This whole sport has grown so much, and there's room for so many different games. Perhaps in the future, one-design offshore classes will become predominant. And I don't think that's necessarily a bad thing. As I remember sailing in one-design classes, you spend more time and effort tuning up than you do in a custom boat, because in a custom boat you think, Well, the boat's good or it isn't good. But when you're sailing week in and week out against boats of the same type, you do anything for an edge.

In Lasers, I remember, they took them apart, trying to find something. So the one-design rules have to be awfully good, and the competition is bound to get more arduous. It's going to make better sailors of the people who are racing the boats, if they can stand losing without having an alibi.

I remember you saying that you believe a lot of people would rather race by rating.

There are a lot of people who like to race by rating, I'm sure, because the sting of defeat is not so great. You always have oodles of excuses, you know: small boat, not my weather, and so on. I would say that handicap offshore racing is a relatively low level of competition, compared with one-design.

Do you think the boatbuilders are setting up a market for one-design?

Absolutely. Having been in the boat business, I know the best thing in the world a boatbuilder can do is establish a proprietary product like the Laser. That way, all he has to do is maintain the same standards for all boats. And he can charge whatever he wants, because no one's competing with him in the same marketplace. They make money on that sort of thing, whereas in building Lightnings or Flying Dutchmans or a class that anyone can build, there's no money in it at all, and there's no promotional budget available, no marketing, no advertising—not even any dealers usually, since there's no room for a dealer markup. This makes it very, very difficult to buy a new custom ocean racer. You have to go to a designer and you have to get a builder, and you don't know what it's going to cost and you don't know whether it's going to be good or not, because you're building a new design. If you buy a J-24, you know what you get; or a Laser, Windsurfer, Sunfish, or Hobie Cat.

So offshore racing is dominated by the

Above: *J-24s battle for clear air at the midwinter regatta in Key West. The J-24 is one of the most popular new one-design cruising classes. Right: Windsurfer champion Matt Schweitzer. Overleaf: Windsurfing has become one of the most popular forms of sailing, another example of one-design success.*

proprietary products. They're also easier to buy and sell.

Let's talk a little about mental preparation. How do you psych yourself?

I stay psyched up all the time. My two sports teams play every day, and I take the role of underdog, so for me it's nothing to be psyched. At least when we're racing it's only once every two weeks or once a weekend.

How about for the circuit? When do you start getting ready mentally?

For races like the Southern Ocean Racing Conference I don't get ready until I get down there, the day before the race. Having an excellent crew and an excellent captain helps, so I stay away from the details and concentrate on the competition.

Do you get nervous before you go out racing?

I used to get tremendously nervous; not as much anymore. Let's face it: I'm fidgety and high-strung. Years ago I used to have a bad case of nerves, and a lot of times I would clutch up. I can remember sailing in a boat one time and my foot started shaking uncontrollably, so I almost fell out of the hiking straps. It was a Sears semifinals, and I had to pass a boat to win. I didn't.

I guess I was so intense in sailing that I clutched there more than in any other area. It's one of the worst habits you can have, because if you're going to clutch in a tight sailing situation, then you will in other situations too—in an automobile, for example, when another car is coming at you.

There are a lot of guys who have that problem. How can you overcome that?

You have to work hard on it, the same way you work on quitting smoking or biting your fingernails. It doesn't hurt either to tell yourself that this race is not that important, that you're going to have a good time. But the real solution is confidence, and that comes with experience and hard work. Then, once you overcome the problem in sailing, it will be a lot easier to overcome it in other areas as well.

What are the important factors a sailor should weigh in looking toward the next year's campaign or the next two years'?

It depends on the sailor's budget, the amount of time he can devote to his racing, how important it is to him in the overall scheme of things. If he is a beginner, he could be shooting to be in the top half of his local fleet the next year, and if he has been down at the bottom, that's a very worthwhile and interesting goal. I don't think you ought to set unrealistically high goals for yourself. It's disappointing if you don't make them.

So you should set a goal. . . .

You don't really have to, but I think it's always more fun to have something in mind that you want to accomplish. If you don't have a goal, it's harder to achieve something.

And your goals—how do you go about planning them each year?

I sit down and think about a year in advance as to what events we're going to attend. After the America's Cup, though, it was a pretty easy year. You build up to it, and then it's best, I think, to take a little time off to yourself. Relax a bit.

How long can you compete for? Some athletes go for a year at a time, then rest. What about you, and other sailors?

It depends on the situation. You have to pace yourself. Sailing is so varied that it's like comparing a sprinter and a marathon runner. You have to pace yourself so that you'll peak when it's most important, and that varies with the type of event you're in.

What about the question of how much time to devote to sailing? Some people seem to get hooked on the sport and lose a sense of pro-

portion. They allow it to rule their lives.

It can be a problem. I would have to say that your business comes first. If you want to give your full time to sailing, you can sail twelve hours a day, three hundred sixty-five days a year, and you can compete in a regatta somewhere every weekend. It's a great field to be in, even though I would caution young people who are thinking about it. It's not as much fun when you do it for a living as when you do it for a hobby. I think if you asked anyone over forty who

has spent his career in it—particularly in the racing area (I'm not talking about yacht brokerage)—you'll find a lot of heartaches.

So if it's not going to be your vocation, then you shouldn't give it more importance than it really has. One of the unhealthy things today, I think, is that many people spend more time playing than working. I've spent a lot of time sailing, but I've spent a lot more time working, and had I not been successful in business, I could never have achieved success in sailing. It took money, and that came from my business. Your career provides for your sailing, so your career should come first.

I find that sailing is great, but a big part is getting around and meeting people and seeing different places. I'd never been to Mackinac Island, for example, before we raced there last summer.

You have the best of all worlds. You're really more like a teacher—a teacher and coach—particularly since so many of your goals have already been achieved. I think that's great. You don't have to prove anything; you can go out and really enjoy it. Share your knowledge with others.

That kind of life is a lot more interesting than that of a sailmaker, who is dealing with all the customers who'd like to blame the fact that they're not winning on their sailmaker. You can get out and race, and somebody's going to be last; you can't blame that on the sails.

One last question. What do you see for the future of twelve-meter racing?

I'd like to see a twelve-meter world championship held the year before the America's Cup—a fleet race off Newport. It would be a great opportunity for yachtsmen from all over the world to get together and exchange ideas. And it would have to make the America's Cup a better competition.

Jobson sets up self-tailing running backstay winch.

Part 2

Boat Speed

boat-handling techniques for every racer

Tuning and Balance

To win any sailboat race, your boat must be in top condition. Its bottom should first be fair and then smoothed out, ensuring that it flows through the water easily. Its centerboard or keel and rudder have to be fair and in the right positions, for proper balance. It's imperative to find out exactly when the rudder is amidships and to mark it at that point. The best way is to have the boat hauled out of the water and make a mark on the helm. Or send someone into the water to line up the rudder amidships and put a mark on the wheel at that point. Set marks on the wheel at, say, one-degree increments, so that you know exactly how much helm is used.

Probably the best rig a sailboat could have is none at all. The smaller and lighter the rig, the faster the boat will be. Nevertheless, it is generally better to rig your boat with slightly heavier equipment than to chance a breakdown with light equipment, particularly on offshore yachts.

The rigging should be set up to allow for maximum speed and power in the sails. For finding out just how your boat should be set up, good starting sources are your sailmaker, boatbuilder, and designer. Basic suggestions they make will probably work well.

The Mast

A great deal of study has gone into finding the best mast shape. Although there are theories that call for turbulence generators on the front part of the spar to break the wind before it gets to the sails, the consensus seems to favor a smooth mast, which allows the wind to flow around it easily into the sail. One thing is clear: the less windage, the faster the boat.

Boats sail best when their masts are straight athwartships, so set your mast up as straight as you can get it. You can check its straightness by hanging a weight on a light string from the top of the mast and observing how the string comes to rest. Ideally it should be right next to the mast, neither fore nor aft.

Sight up the mast to keep it straight as you adjust the shrouds. They should be tightened about the same as those on the boats you will be racing against. A tension meter will guide you in putting equal tension on both sides.

The spreaders control side bend—the longer the spreaders, the more you can increase sidestay tension and the less the bend in the mast. It is important for the spreaders to be tightly secured to the mast; otherwise they can break, since there are many forces pushing and pulling at them. To minimize the force of the wind, the spreaders should be a streamlined airfoil shape, much like an airplane wing. Spreaders and fittings on the mast should be faired in, so that the wind flows around them easily. Halyards should not be left to flap in the breeze.

As a rule, spreaders should be fitted so as to keep the shrouds in the same plane in which they would be without spreaders. Pushing the spreaders forward causes the tip of the mast to go forward, whereas moving the spreaders aft causes the middle of the mast to go forward and the tip of the mast to go aft.

There should be absolutely no play be-

Opening spread: *Overhead view reveals crew in position as* Courageous *sails upwind in seventeen knots of breeze during fourth America's Cup race against* Australia. *Turner is at helm, Jobson just in front.*

45

tween the mast and the mast partner. By pulling blocks out from the front of the mast partner, a common technique in boats ranging from 470s to twelve-meters, you allow more mast bend. Blocking the front part of the mast restricts its bend.

Balance

A boat should sail on the angle of heel that allows it to move fastest through the water. This is called "sailing on its lines." In a Laser the angle of heel is between zero and ten degrees, depending on the wave conditions. On many offshore yachts, the angle of heel may be twenty-five to thirty degrees, because the boat rides relatively high in the water and can accommodate that much higher a waterline when it heels over.

Your objective is to sail with a long waterline, keeping the water flowing evenly off the stern. To accomplish this, the crew's weight should be distributed so that it is heaviest in the widest part of the boat, normally as close to the center as possible. If the crew's weight is too far aft, the stern will sag; too far forward and the water will separate from the hull too far forward (Diagram 1), forming a vacuum underneath the boat that produces centerboard cavitation. It is critically important to keep a uniform water pressure on the centerboard, since it is this force that neutralizes the sidewise force of the wind in the sails and allows the wind's forward force to push the boat forward. (Diagram 2)

Ideally, then, a boat should sail both at the optimal angle of heel (on its lines) and balanced fore and aft by the crew's weight. However, most sailboats sail best when they have about five degrees of windward helm. Windward helm is that characteristic of a boat whereby it heads up into the wind when the helm is left untended. In other words, the boat is slightly unbalanced, for

1. Balance Fore and Aft

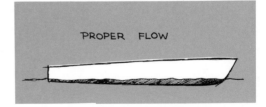

PROPER FLOW

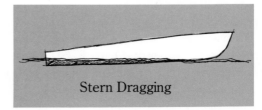

Stern Dragging

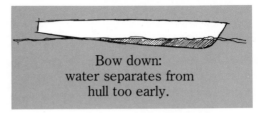

Bow down:
water separates from
hull too early.

2. Cavitation and Its Effect

If board
cavitates
sailboat
will sideslip.

Cavitation

46

Two unbalanced boats. Top: *Heeled over too far, this boat has exposed, cavitating keel.* Bottom: *This Lehman 10 crew needs to get weight closer together and farther over the side to flatten boat.*

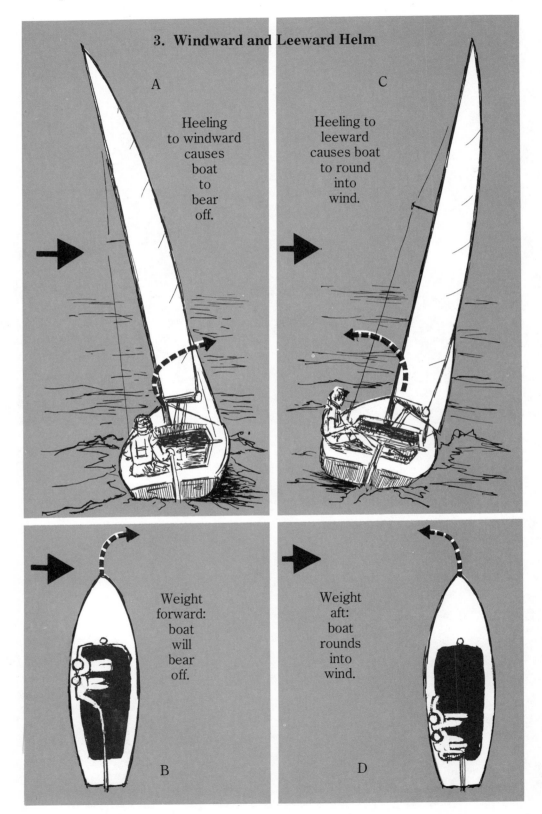

3. Windward and Leeward Helm

A

Heeling to windward causes boat to bear off.

C

Heeling to leeward causes boat to round into wind.

Weight forward: boat will bear off.

B

Weight aft: boat rounds into wind.

D

a balanced boat will sail along with no change in course if you leave the rudder uncontrolled.

Windward helm is the product of all the factors that go into balancing—or in this case, slightly unbalancing—a boat, from rigging to crew weight distribution (side to side and fore and aft) to sail trim. (Diagram 3) Often in coaching sailors we find that one of the major reasons they are not pointing when they should be is that they simply are not steering the boat up into the wind. Windward helm will help this problem.

Windward helm can be induced by shifting crew weight aft, by heeling the boat to leeward, or by raking the mast aft, so that you have more power in your sails aft of the centerline of your boat. (Diagram 4) Likewise, shifting crew weight forward,

heeling the boat to windward, or moving the mast forward creates leeward helm, or at least reduces windward helm. Sailing downwind on *Courageous,* we pulled the top of the mast forward about a foot and a half to reduce our windward helm. It can also be reduced by easing the sails or hiking the boat flatter. On *Courageous* we sailed upwind with five of our crew in hiking straps to help keep the boat slightly flatter.

Incidentally, it is important when hiking to get away from the boat as far as possible. A study at MIT a number of years ago found that for every inch a crew hikes out, the boat effectively gains three pounds of righting moment. If you are on a trapeze boat, learn to stand on your toes with your feet close together so that you are farther away from the boat. Weight jackets are always better than weight pants, because they get the weight farther from the boat.

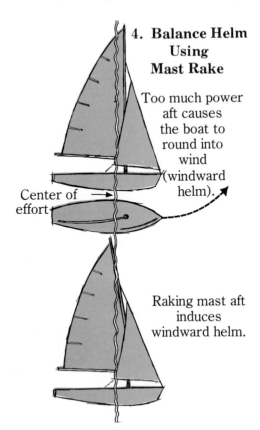

4. Balance Helm Using Mast Rake

Too much power aft causes the boat to round into wind (windward helm).

Center of effort

Raking mast aft induces windward helm.

Sail Trim

After the proper preparation of the boat, sail trim is the most important factor in achieving good boat speed. In sailing together, we have used a number of sail-trim techniques that work well. Ted is probably one of the outstanding sail trimmers in the world—an impressive achievement considering the fact that he is not a sailmaker. The reason for his superiority in this field is simple: he sails more than most people, and when he does he is always concentrating on how the sails are working.

We don't think we've ever spent more than thirty seconds sailing together when Ted hasn't called for some sort of sail adjustment. Sails have to be worked con-

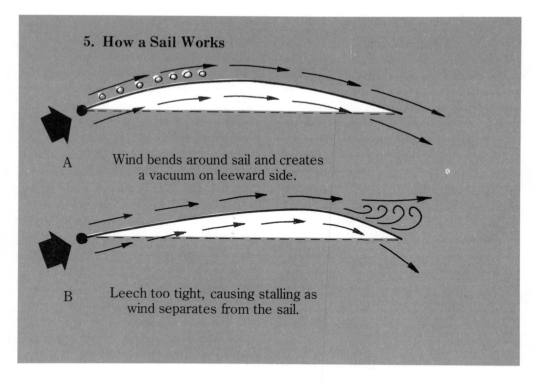

5. How a Sail Works

A — Wind bends around sail and creates a vacuum on leeward side.

B — Leech too tight, causing stalling as wind separates from the sail.

stantly to conform to the different wave and wind patterns. Cleating the sheets down is a mistake, because the wind changes continuously through two or three knots, depending on the size of waves, your pitching moment through the water, and the temperature of the air or the water. You must change gears and adjust your sails accordingly. This is the real secret of sailing a boat well.

No matter what sail you may be flying—mainsail, genoa, spinnaker, or even staysail—it works on the same principle: wind bends around the sail, causing a vacuum on the outer edge. (Diagram 5) The boat pushes forward to fill this vacuum, so a sail propels a boat not only by catching the wind but by displacing wind it doesn't catch. If the wind bends too much in flowing around the sail, there will be too much of a vacuum too close to the sail, back drafts will result, and the boat will "stall out." On the other

hand, if too much wind is caught in the sail, the boat will heel too much, overpowered. You should have as much power in the sails as possible and still keep the boat "sailing on its lines." The power in your sails should bring you to this optimal angle of heel earliest. It is just as important to have the proper amount of draft in a sail as it is to have that draft properly positioned (see below). The trick is to have as much sail area as possible exposed to the wind while at the same time having the shape that creates the most power.

Mainsails

All mainsails are cut with luff round in them—a curved forward edge. Attaching a curved edge to a straight mast causes draft in the sail. (Diagram 6) Sails are made to have draft in them, particularly at a panel called the draft control, along the foot. This

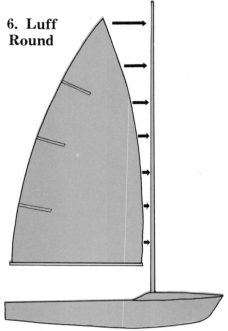

6. Luff Round

Tension on head and foot creates draft in sail.

permits a sail with draft to be rigged on a stiff boom. Most boats sail best with stiff booms, using draft-control panels on the mainsail to create draft. However, if the mast is bending fore and aft too much, it may help to use a softer boom.

Look at a sail from the bottom of the boat and sight up toward the head of the mast. Your goal is to have the maximum amount of draft, or camber, in the sail halfway between the ends of the boom, or fifty percent of the way aft. (Diagram 7) When the sail is shaped this way, it is curved to displace wind and exposed to catch wind in just the proper balance.

Sailing with the midshipmen at the Naval Academy, Gary was trying to show the crew how to recognize when draft is fifty percent of the way aft. As he was explaining the point to a midshipman named David Bissot, the idea struck Gary of drawing a line in the middle of the boom, angled straight for the head of the sail. This "Biss mark"

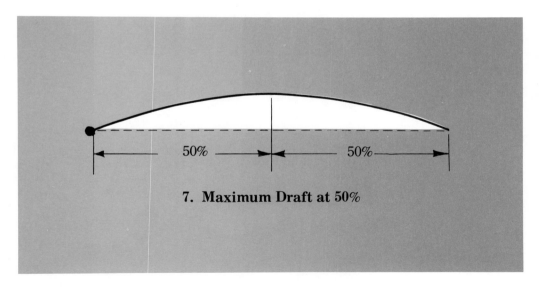

50% — 50%

7. Maximum Draft at 50%

8. The Biss Mark

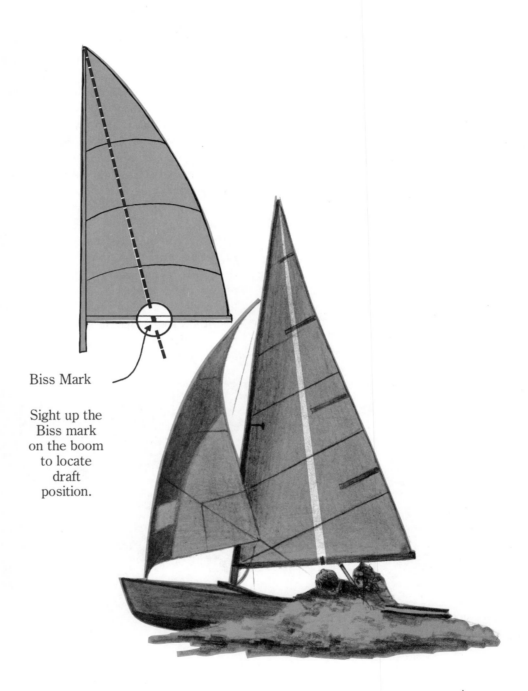

Biss Mark

Sight up the
Biss mark
on the boom
to locate
draft
position.

points right to the spot where the maximum draft in the sail should be. (Diagram 8)

Reference marks like this help you see what you are looking for. Many sailmakers put what are called "speed stripes"—horizontal black bands—on a sail to facilitate determining the shape of the sail.

Whenever you put tension on a sail, the draft moves in that direction. So to pull draft forward in a sail (Diagram 9), straighten the mast or tighten the downhaul or cunningham. Tightening the cunningham moves

draft forward by increasing tension along the luff. At the same time, it stiffens and flattens the middle part of the leech of the sail. To move draft aft in a sail (Diagram 10), ease the cunningham and trim the main harder, thus tightening and hooking the leech of the sail. Or tighten the outhaul, bending the mast to lower draft in the sail and also to reduce draft as the sail is flattened.

As a general rule, observe the top of the leech of your sail. The top batten should be

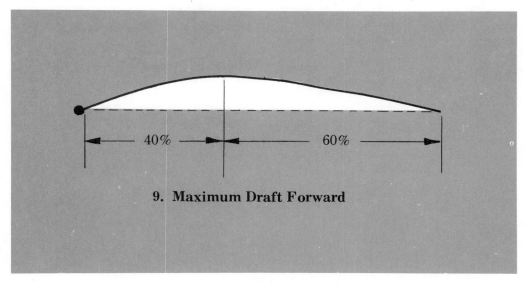

40% 60%

9. Maximum Draft Forward

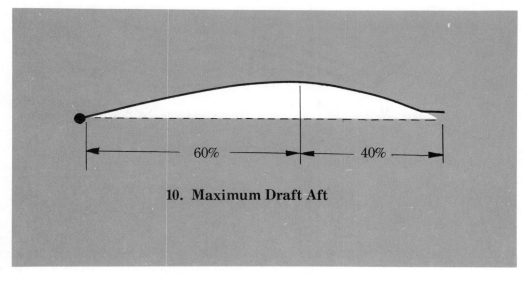

60% 40%

10. Maximum Draft Aft

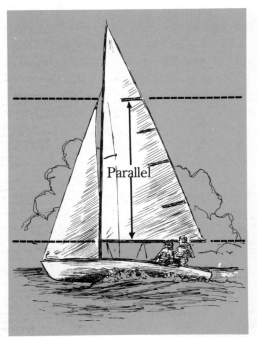

11. Top Batten Parallel to Boom

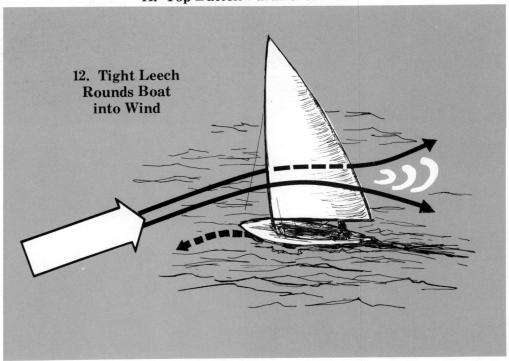

12. Tight Leech Rounds Boat into Wind

Independence sailing to windward with sails perfectly trimmed—leeches of main and genoa nearly parallel.

about parallel to the boom. (Diagram 11) If the top batten is hooking to windward, it is an indication that the draft in your sails is too far aft—or in other words, that you are slightly overtrimmed, causing the boat to tend to round up into the wind. (Diagram 12) If, on the other hand, your batten seems to be falling off, then you are under-trimmed, with draft too far forward.

It may be helpful to use telltales to improve your ability to trim sails. When you are making better speed than your competition, note where your telltales are streaming and trim to that point. Normally when you are going fast the telltales will stream aft, but not always.

Courageous *on port, crossing* Australia, *whose sails are poorly trimmed. Compare the nearly parallel line of* Independence's *main and genoa leeches* (previous page) *to* Australia's *here.*

Boomvang

The boomvang is a useful tool, and in small boats "vang sheeting" is becoming more popular. By keeping the end of the boom on a constant plane, it allows one to sheet the main as if there were no traveler. The mainsheet moves the boom in and out, and the vang keeps the leech tight and puts power in the sail. A boomvang can also be used to keep the top batten parallel to the boom.

Vang sheeting works well in high-performance boats that plane quickly. It does not work if you are overpowered, because the boat will heel more as the mainsail is eased out. In this case the vang should be eased off slightly, so that the top part of the leech begins to twist or open up, spilling wind out of the top of the sail. (Diagram 13)

13. Boomvang

A
Hard vang;
tight
leech

B
Soft vang;
loose
leech

Jibs and Genoas

Jibs and genoas are trimmed like a mainsail: once again, the maximum amount of draft should be about fifty percent of the way aft. The bottom part of the leech should be hooked slightly to windward of the top of the sail. The jib should be trimmed inboard of the boat until you begin to get backwind in the main, at which point the jib lead should be moved outboard.

The jib is worked in conjunction with the main and should be constantly tended by the sail trimmer. As a rule, the leech of the jib should form a parallel line with the luff of the mainsail. By watching the slot between the mainsail and the jib, try to get the leech of the jib to conform with the main in this way.

When the apparent wind is forward of 135 degrees, the jib works best trimmed on the leeward side of the boat. Once the wind is aft of about 135 degrees, the jib is more effective trimmed to windward. To trim a jib to windward, get the clew of the sail as far as possible away from the boat. If the jib has a tendency to luff, ease the sail out, letting the clew go forward. This will help the sail to fill sooner. (Diagram 14)

All boats have some jibstay sag, and the only reliable way to minimize it is to be sure your sailmaker adjusts your luff round in the jib to account for it. If you need power in the sail, you should try to remove as much sag from the jibstay as you can. As the boat becomes overpowered, let the jibstay sag off slightly.

To determine how much jibstay sag you have, attach a halyard to the bow of your boat just at the tack of the jib. Place a telltale in the middle of this halyard. It will flow in the direction of the wind and will indicate to you how much jibstay sag you have, whether it be a few inches, six inches, or a foot and a half.

14. Jib Trim
Wind aft of 135°;
jib is winged
to windward.

If jib has tendency to
luff, ease the clew forward.

Wind forward of 135°;
trim jib to leeward.

To prevent the sail from flapping around in case the jibsheet breaks, which could cause a considerable loss of time and distance, set in an extra jibsheet around a spare winch. On *Tenacious* an extra sheet for this purpose is always attached immediately after tacking in any breeze over about twelve knots.

In shifty winds trimming the jib in coordination with the helmsman can be a challenging experience. On most boats there is a constant battle between the tailer and helmsman, so once these two crew members can work together, your boat has an edge over the rest of the fleet.

The tailer has to watch what the wind is doing. If the wind fairs and the boat is lifted, the jib needs adjusting or it will be overtrimmed, forcing the boat away from the wind. The tailer should first ease out the sail, so that the boat increases speed and the helmsman need not use much rudder to bring the boat up. Then, as the boat heads up, the tailer trims the sail in slowly.

If the boat is headed, the trailer may trim his sail in to force the bow away from the wind.

In checking the trim of a genoa, luff the boat slowly into the wind. As the sails luff, all the telltales should luff at the same time. If you find that the top telltale luffs first, you need to trim the leech tighter, powering up the sail. If this adjustment is only a minor one, take the genoa halyard up tighter. For a major adjustment, you will have to move the jib lead forward, powering up the leech. If you find the bottom telltale is luffing first, you should move the jib lead aft. Your goal is to get the jib to luff evenly, ensuring that your leech is standing up properly and giving the maximum amount of power in the sail.

Spinnakers

For an effective spinnaker it is necessary first of all to be sure that the sail itself is stable, since an unstable sail bounces around and loses power. Stability comes from a heavy cloth, with its greater density to keep wind from escaping through the sail. So you should look for a heavy spinnaker. Of course, in light winds lighter sails are needed to get the spinnaker to fly.

Trimming a spinnaker is much like trimming either the genoa or the mainsail. Once again, the maximum amount of draft should be in the middle, or about fifty percent of the way aft. Haul the spinnaker halyard all the way to the head of the mast, although if you are having difficulty flying the spinnaker you may want to ease the spinnaker halyard off a few inches to get the head away from the mast. Be sure that your halyard for the spinnaker is strong enough; a weak halyard will stretch when a puff hits, absorbing energy that should be going into the sail. It is also a good idea to have the halyard wrapped around a winch, or at least

*Skipper sits to leeward so crew can ride trapeze for quick hiking
in a puff and have a better vantage point for trimming the spinnaker.*

secured through a block—a further reinforcement.

To check whether the draft is in the middle of the spinnaker (Diagram 15), first see if both clews of the sail make a line parallel to the water. If one clew is higher than the other, pole height needs adjusting. Lower your pole to move draft forward in the sail, for more power; raise the pole to move draft aft, to flatten it for less power. If you have a center seam cut into your spinnaker, this should be about perpendicular to the horizon. If the center seam meets the water at an angle, your pole is not adjusted properly. Try to have your spinnaker pole extending from the mast at a right angle; the farther away from the mast it is, the easier

to fly the spinnaker. The trick to good spinnaker trim is to get the spinnaker away from the boat as far as possible, so that the air flows around the sail more freely, giving more power.

It is important for a spinnaker trimmer to watch all parts of the sail to see that it is trimmed correctly. The luff, the leech, and the foot should all have about equal tension. The sail should luff about in the middle of the luff. Telltales on the luff of a spinnaker are useful and should be placed at equal intervals from the top to the bottom. Three is probably the best number, about six to twelve inches aft of the luff of the sail. (Diagram 16)

The spinnaker trimmer must be in a good

15. The Spinnaker

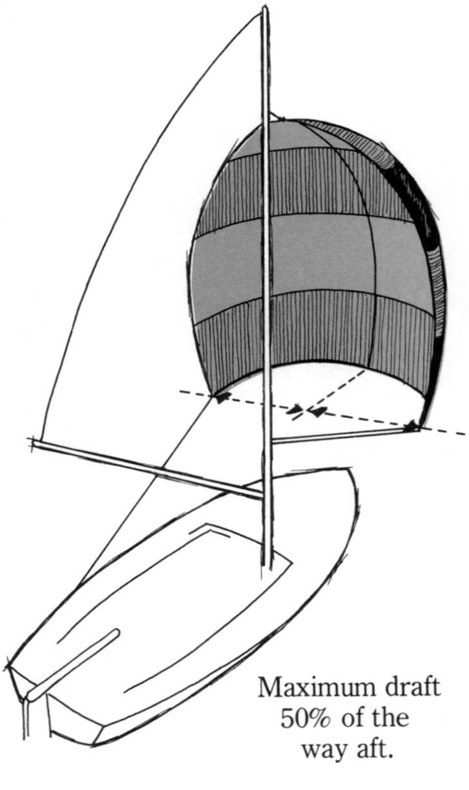

Maximum draft 50% of the way aft.

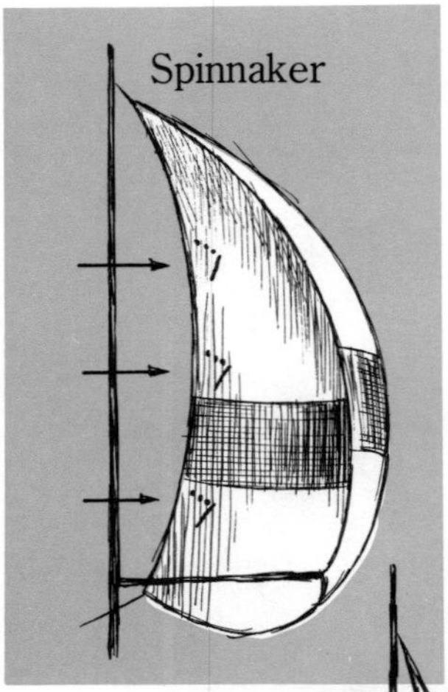

Spinnaker

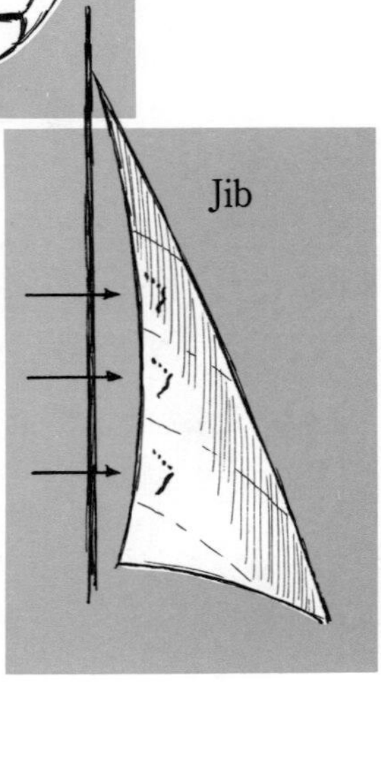

16. Telltales on Spinnaker and Jib

Jib

position to see the sail. Normally, this is well forward on the windward side of the boat. In a Flying Dutchman, the crew will be out on a trapeze to watch the spinnaker. The skipper sits to leeward to balance the boat if necessary.

The spinnaker must be played constantly to keep the maximum amount of draft in the sail. Since the air bends more slowly in a spinnaker, compared with the main or jib, this sail can be flown with more draft.

Choking a spinnaker helps make the boat more stable. Move the sheet lead forward to tighten the leech. If you cannot move the leads, consider trimming the spinnaker under the boom to choke the sail. To free it up, trim the spinnaker over the boom.

Bloopers

Spinnaker staysails and bloopers stabilize a boat downwind by helping to balance it. They work best when the apparent wind is aft of about 140 degrees.

The secret in flying a blooper is getting it as far as possible away from the boat and spinnaker. The blooper should not be flown if it will overlap the spinnaker, because if it does, both sails will likely collapse. Use the longest possible pendant on the tack of the blooper to get it away from the boat. Trim to the stern, well outboard of the spinnaker sheet. Ease off the halyard so that the blooper is about three or four feet off the water and is still filled, and at the same time ease the sheet as much as you can.

Observe where the halyard of the blooper is streaming. (Diagram 17) If it is about twenty degrees forward of a perpendicular line drawn from the mast, the blooper is pulling the boat more to the side than forward and should be taken down. This is the time to set a normal staysail. Staysails draw best when tacked aft to open the slot between the staysail and the spinnaker. The

Tenacious *flying spinnaker and blooper.*
The trick to flying a blooper is to get
it as far from the boat as possible.

staysail should be trimmed like a genoa, so that it luffs evenly. If the sail luffs at the top first, the staysail lead should be more forward. If the sail luffs at the bottom first, the lead should be moved aft to get it away from the spinnaker. As long as the sail is filled, staysail leads should be trimmed as far outboard as possible.

17. Flying Bloopers

20°

Wind Sheer

Wind sheer occurs when the wind aloft is blowing in a different direction from the wind close to the water. (Diagram 18) It is more commonly encountered on boats with tall masts, but is experienced by any boat. The streams where jets fly may be flowing in an entirely different direction from the winds at ground level. Wind sheer can be so bad that the masthead calls for a spinnaker with the wind abeam or behind the beam, and yet down low you need a jib. In these circumstances, as much of the sail as possible

18. Wind Sheer

Apparent wind farther aft at top of the sail

should be drawing properly. Stay with the jib if the wind is fairer aloft than it is down low. In this case, move the jib lead aft a little and ease out the main a little, so that the top of the sail works with the bottom. Twist the leeches of both sails if you are headed aloft. If you tack over, then the wind will be fairer down low than it is aloft. In these instances, trim your main fairly tight, move the traveler way up to windward, and close up the leech on your jib, if you're using one.

Marking

Every sail trimmer should keep a marking pen with him to make reference marks when sailing. The mainsheet, jibsheet, and spinnaker sheet should all be marked at the point where they meet the appropriate fitting on deck to produce a given point of sail. Likewise, cunninghams, barber haulers, halyards, and guys should be marked for their proper positions in various wind conditions. Also, the deck should be marked with reference points to indicate when leads are properly positioned. And all these marks should be reviewed whenever you sail. A system of marks is used on all Ted's boats, because it is often difficult for crew members to remember exactly where to position the various lines. By giving you a reference when you are not sure where to trim—particularly helpful during a complicated maneuver—a marking system keeps the crew sailing the boat on track and at maximum speed. If you are going through a set of tacks, you will need three marks: one for the optimal trim, one for the maximum trim, and one for the maximum ease.

Sail Selection

As you learn which sails to use on your boat, put a list of them in a conspicuous place, so that you know exactly at what apparent windspeed and what apparent wind angle to use them. For example, we used this headsail chart on *Tenacious:*

    2–5 knots: light number 1
    5–12 knots: medium number 1
    12–20 knots: heavy number 1
    20–25 knots: number 2
    25–33 knots: number 3
    32 knots and up: number 4

Of course, a chart such as this is only a reference; the trick is to observe how you are doing at a given time, so that you can make adjustments. On *Courageous* we had computer values for various wind strengths and directions, telling us which sails to use when. We were often able to exceed the values, because we were improving our standard of performance. You may experience the same thing in your own boat as conditions vary and you learn to sail the boat better.

Steering

In small boats the best sailors seem to "wear their boats," working them through the waves by steering as if their minds were moving the boats along the course. When you are steering a sailboat well, it becomes an extension of you, and there is probably no more enjoyable sensation in sailing. To steer well takes practice and experience, but by working hard and concentrating on the course, you will acquire the skill in a short time.

The helmsman controls the boat by controlling the helm. Don't let the boat control you. Be sure that your steering mechanism is sturdy, particularly the pintles and gudgeons; sailboats cannot have strong-enough steering gear. Better to have equipment that is a little heavy than to risk a breakdown. The hiking stick must swivel easily and be strong enough not to break. It must also be long enough to allow the helmsman to hike as far away from the boat as possible.

Keep a good grip on the wheel or tiller, so that it doesn't slip. Any action given to a rudder should be a direct action from the helmsman's arm. And every action of the hiking stick should go directly to the tiller

Finn sailor Pat Healy shows good hiking position: legs bent at
a ninety-degree angle, weight evenly distributed side to side,
and hiking stick kept in the same plane as the tiller.

and the rudder: the rudder, tiller, or wheel should have absolutely no play in it. On larger boats, the bigger the wheel the easier it is to steer. A large wheel makes it easier to stay in the groove longer, giving greater leverage to prevent oversteering.

When you're steering, stay organized in your boat and try to steer from about the same position. Keep the tiller and hiking stick on the same plane. It is interesting to note how different sailors from around the world steer. Sailors from the East Coast usually hold the hiking stick perpendicular to the tiller. West Coast sailors hold the hiking stick so that it angles down to the tiller, causing oversteering because the arms are not well braced. European sailors steer across their bodies, holding the hiking stick with the arm about parallel to the tiller. This technique, providing both greater stability and greater feel, is rapidly becoming popular in the United States.

In larger boats, many helmsmen have felt it is best to sit to leeward, so that they get to watch the jib. But the best helmsmen stand up and steer to windward, because that way they can see both sails working together and at the same time watch the angle of heel, together with the wind and

Opposite: *Laser sailor fully extended to keep boat flat; body straight to stay out of the water.* Above: Courageous *crewmen in hiking straps. Boat's separate rudders visible through water.*

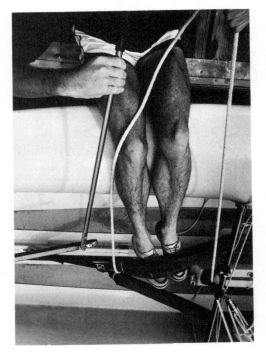

Above *and* left: *Two views of proper hiking position.* Above: *Keep a firm grip on hiking stick.* Left: *Note hiking stick, mainsheet, and legs in hiking straps are all about parallel.*

waves as they are coming across the water.

There are two schools of thought in steering: to keep a dead helm, not steering at all, and to steer a lot. The conditions determine which method to use. In relatively steady wind and flat water, a boat has a tendency to slow down whenever you move the tiller, so steering a lot is to be avoided. In choppy conditions, however, you may find that you have to steer more to maneuver the boat around the waves. Similarly, you may have to steer more in puffy wind conditions.

In lighter boats, such as Lasers, it has become popular to steer so much that the boat is almost sculled upwind. But it is worth noting that the first Laser world champions, John Bertrand and Peter Commette, steer very little.

A perennial steering question is whether to drive (sailing with the sails full) or to pinch (sailing with the sails luffing). You need to practice searching for the fine line between sailing directly on course and going for speed. As a rule, pinching is better in flat water as long as the boat is kept on its lines. As the boat becomes overpowered, play the sails, easing them out in the puffs. In these conditions, keeping the boat on its lines is the most important factor in good steering. Playing the sails and feathering (pinching) slightly will help to do this. When the waves are short and choppy, drive the boat to keep up speed. In a chop, power in the sails should be well forward. Steer around the waves so that your bow never goes into a wave at a right angle.

Maneuvering

The faster you maneuver a boat, the faster it loses speed, so to keep up momentum, move the rudder slowly. A sailboat will usually turn a complete circle in about a one-and-a-half-boat-length radius. Turning any faster will kill speed unnecessarily. Whenever you are maneuvering a sailboat, whether to accelerate, tack, jibe, head up, or bear off, the most important thing is to have as much speed as possible.

Acceleration/Deceleration

The heavier the boat, the longer it takes to get it moving. To get a twelve-meter up to full speed from a dead stop takes about a minute and a half. In a Laser, on the other hand, you can go from a dead stop to full speed in about fifteen or twenty seconds.

No boat will maneuver until it starts to move. Trim your sails in and pull your tiller in the opposite direction, so that the two forces help the boat to start moving forward. But try to use as little helm as possible, so that the rudder does not break the boat's forward momentum. Continue to adjust the sails to complement the motion and movement of the boat, depending on the course you intend to take. If the boat starts rounding up too quickly, ease the sails to bear off. Keep the boat on its best sailing lines. A boat that is heeling too much is out of balance and will be slow to move. If it is a boat that should be sailed flat, keep it flat or heeled slightly to leeward, so that the sail takes shape. Never let a boat heel to windward when you are trying to accelerate.

As the boat starts moving, sail in a straight line for a distance of one to three boat lengths before starting to bear off to attain full speed. Once the boat is up to full speed, you can begin to maneuver.

Many sailors concentrate so much on speed that they have a hard time learning to slow down when they have to. A good way to do it is not slowing down but adding more distance. If, for example, you are coming into a leeward mark and find yourself trapped outside a boat, you can improve your position by making a large alteration in course to leeward and then sharpening up. You sail an extra distance, without losing speed, and round the leeward mark so that you end up on the inside windward quarter of the boat ahead after the rounding.

Tacking Lines

Every sailboat can use a set of tacking lines. (Diagram 19) Drawn on the deck, these lines are easy to mark and are valuable references when you are sighting other boats, ahead or behind, or you are determining who is going to cross whom in a crossing situation.

To mark the tacking lines, start by running a string down the center of the boat. Using a protractor to measure the angle, draw a line perpendicular to the string, then another line perpendicular to the first one. Then mark a forty-five degree angle, bisecting the perpendicular formed by the two lines. You now have three lines: one running fore and aft, one perpendicular to fore and aft, and one right between the two. These will become the basis for the tacking lines.

Knowing what angle your boat normally tacks through, be it a hundred degrees in light air, ninety in medium, or eighty or less in higher winds and flat water, draw your tacking lines accordingly. For example, on *Courageous* we set up three tacking lines, at ninety, eighty, and seventy degees. If the boat was tacking through seventy degrees, we knew we were on the lay line when the mark lined up on the seventy-degree tacking line.

For determining whether a boat to leeward is ahead of or behind you as you are about to tack across it, you need another set of lines, half the angle of the first set— or in our case, forty-five, forty, and thirty-five degrees. Likewise, to determine whether a boat to windward is ahead of or behind you, you need an identical set of lines on the other side. Using the lines, you simply choose the appropriate one—half the angle through which you are tacking—and sight down it. If the boat is ahead of the line as you extend it, it will pass ahead of you; behind and it will pass behind you; in both cases assuming that the speed of both boats remains constant.

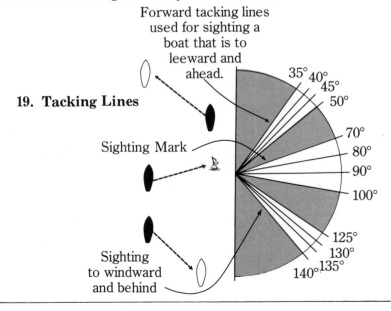

Forward tacking lines used for sighting a boat that is to leeward and ahead.

19. Tacking Lines

Sighting Mark

35° 40° 45° 50° 70° 80° 90° 100° 125° 130° 135° 140°

Sighting to windward and behind

Hand-Bearing Compass

Ted discovered several years ago that the hand-bearing compass is a valuable tool in determining how our boat is fairing in relation to others. You can use it in a number of ways.

First, by taking bearings on the bow of a rival boat at intervals of, say, one minute, you can see how much distance that boat has gained or lost in relation to you. If one boat length equals eight degrees, for example, and you have gained a half degree, you know that you have gained a sixteenth of a boat length. Such a small change is often difficult to discern with the naked eye.

Second, a hand-bearing compass can determine whether you are gaining windward or leeward distance on a rival boat, provided the boats do not alter course. Let's say that sighting through the compass you find it is six degrees from the bow to the stern of a boat to leeward. After sailing for two minutes, you take another reading, and the boat to leeward now bears five and a half degrees, while the bearing on the bow has

Using the hand-bearing compass, tactician Jobson takes a reading on the competition. Distance gained or lost can be measured within three feet.

remained constant. The explanation is that the boats have moved farther apart laterally.

The hand-bearing compass also comes in handy in crossing situations, for determining whether you can get away with a tack on the leeward bow of a converging boat. Check its bearing every fifteen or thirty seconds. If the boat is gaining bearing on you, it will cross ahead of you. If you are gaining bearing on it, you will cross ahead. If the bearing stays constant, you'll have to maneuver to stay clear of each other.

If you find that you can cross the boat by a half boat length, then you also have the room to tack on its lee bow, without being overtaken before you can get up to speed after the tack.

There are a number of hand-bearing compasses on the market. The best ones can be read easily, dampened down so that the compass points do not bounce around. It takes much practice to make accurate readings with the hand-bearing compass, but the practice is worthwhile, because sound decisions on tactics and sail trim depend on a precisely accurate reading of how you're doing.

Tacking

Generally, it takes between one and three boat lengths to tack in winds stronger than five knots, and as much as five to seven boat lengths in winds less than five knots. For this reason, tack only if you are up to full speed, or at least are going as fast as your competition. Never tack if you are going slower than the competition.

Your aim is to keep up as much speed as possible while assuming the new course as quickly as possible. To learn just how to do this, practice with another boat, tacking simultaneously and seeing which boat gains on the other by tacking more slowly or more quickly.

Using your weight, heel the boat slightly to leeward before tacking. As the boat heads into the wind, heel it to windward hard, rolling the boat through the tack. To maintain your speed, use as little helm as you can. As you head into the wind, trim your sails in, keeping them full. In a sloop, you should trim both the main and the jib at the same time. Several years ago, this "roll tacking" was used only in dinghies. Today it works in almost all boats, even in Solings or one-tonners. It's easy and fun and helps to get the boat quickly up to full speed.

Whenever you tack a lot, put more power into your sails, so that you increase your speed sooner. It may help to head down slightly after a tack, close-reaching to accelerate, and then, as your speed increases, to head up to your normal course, all the time playing your sails for maximum speed.

Here is a brief description of what happens onboard *Courageous* during a tack:

First the tactician passes the word to the helmsman and counts down the distance in boat lengths: "Stand by for a tack in two

1.

4.

74

2.

3.

*Roll-tack sequence (view across): 1.)
preparation (boat must be moving at
full speed); 2.) helm goes to leeward,
both sails are trimmed, and crew
hikes boat to windward; 3.) boat rolls
through tack, heels to leeward on
new tack; 4.) as sails fill on new
tack, crew moves to windward side;
5.) after the tack, boat is flattened
for acceleration.*

5.

75

and a half boat lengths . . . two boat lengths . . ." and so on. When it comes time to tack, the helmsman calls "hard-a-lee," giving good warning to the crew that the boat is beginning to turn. At this time the jib is being trimmed in to keep the sail full and help the boat round up into the wind. At the same time, the main traveler is pulled to windward, also helping the boat head up.

As the boat rounds into the wind, the helm is turned faster to get the boat on the new course sooner. The boat is now rounding into the wind more quickly. To bag the main as the sails begin to luff, the permanent backstay is eased off to straighten the mast, and the hydraulic ram on the outhaul is being pumped in. The genoa halyard, the jib cunningham, and the main cunningham are eased off, so that the sails will become fuller when the boat is on its new course.

A tacking line in the middle of the foot of the jib makes it easier to bring the clew of the jib up and around the shrouds and mast. Thanks to a special coating, the sails have less friction as they go around the mast to the other side. As the sails are beginning to fill, one running backstay is eased off while the other is being ground up. (Runners are wound to exert pressure between 8,500 and 10,000 pounds.)

At this time, speed begins to increase, and the traveler is reset to its normal position, the jib cunningham is trimmed back down, the jib halyard is put back up, and the main cunningham goes down. The hydraulic ram on the outhaul goes back out as the permanent backstay comes down to bend the mast once again. Then we are up to full speed and it's time to stand by for a tack once again.

Using Dual Jib Leads When Tacking

If you are using the inboard jib leads on a windward leg, you can pick up speed faster after tacking by using a double-lead system. Set your jib sheets up through the inboard leads. Have a second jib sheet, a changing sheet, set up on each side of the boat and led through the outboard lead.

Just as the jib fills during the tack, hook the changing sheet into the clew of the jib. J-lock-type shackles are helpful in this case. Trim the jib on the outboard lead as the boat accelerates. Once up to full speed, begin trimming the jib to the inboard lead.

Jibing

The time to jibe is when you are moving the fastest, because it's easier to keep wind in your sails and you lose the least distance. In a dinghy the best time to jibe is when you are surfing down a wave with maximum speed, since you have less power in the sails (apparent wind is less) and are therefore most stable. Always keep the boat flat. The centerboard should be down about one-third of the way for control, but too much centerboard will cause the boat to flip over.

Use all your crew, stationing everyone at a different part of the boat. And use marks to indicate how much to ease or trim your guys and sheets. Marks can also tell you how far to dip your spinnaker pole when passing it underneath the forestay.

In jibing with the spinnaker, the trick is to get the spinnaker away from the boat as far as you can before jibing. Before swinging the pole over, trim it all the way aft, so that it is perpendicular to the mast. In this manner you will be able to change course quickly on the new jibe and the spinnaker will not collapse, since it is already on the leeward side of the boat. As the pole comes aft on the new side, the spinnaker will follow automatically.

Try not to jibe the main over until the wind is just passing straight aft of the boat. Jibing too early will collapse the spinnaker. On the other hand, if you are in a circling maneuver at the start, no matter what the boat, throwing the mainsail over early (pre-jibing) will cause the boat to jibe sooner and will round it into the wind, helping you to make a circle quicker. (Diagram 20)

Many sailors lose as much as two boat lengths unnecessarily when jibing, especially in light air, because they make too great a change of course. In winds of five to ten knots, you need to change course only about thirty or forty degrees to jibe. In heavier winds you need to change course only some twenty degrees.

Roll jibing (Diagram 21) will help prevent too great a course change. It works well in dinghies, particularly in light air. First heel the boat to leeward, then heel it hard to windward, so that the main changes sides quickly. In this way you will not have to make a great alteration of course.

Another common error in jibing is forgetting to change hands in holding the sheet

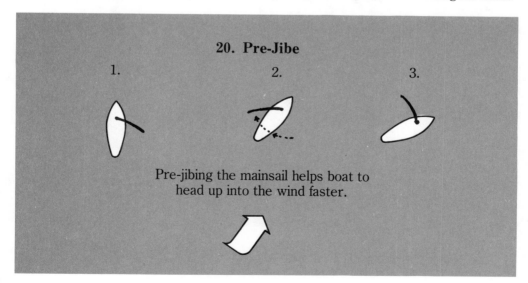

20. Pre-Jibe

1.   2.   3.

Pre-jibing the mainsail helps boat to head up into the wind faster.

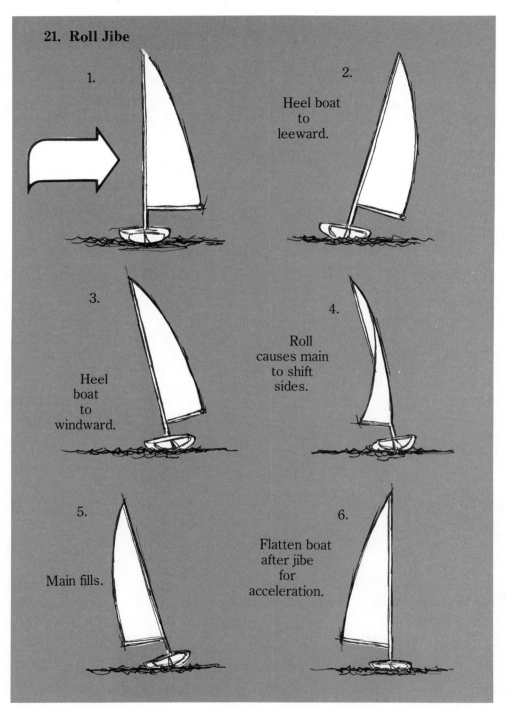

21. Roll Jibe

1.

2. Heel boat to leeward.

3. Heel boat to windward.

4. Roll causes main to shift sides.

5. Main fills.

6. Flatten boat after jibe for acceleration.

and tiller, putting yourself off balance. To avoid this, it may help to switch hands before your jibe.

Use an S-jibe to keep your boat under control when jibing in heavy wind. In heavy-air jibing, the main boom comes over with such force that it goes too far out on the new side and the boat begins to round into the wind. At its worst, this loss of control can capsize dinghies or broach larger keelboats. To stay upright, you must keep the boat under the mast and the boat in balance. An S-jibe can accomplish this.

As you go into an S-jibe, bear off and keep the boat sailing slightly by-the-lee. Keep the main overtrimmed at this time, or if you are sailing with a spinnaker, choke it down slightly by overtrimming the guy and sheet. Then, as the mainsail is coming across the boat, steer back in the direction in which the main is going. This change of course reduces the power in the sail and

1.

2.

3.

4.

S-jibe sequence (view across): 1.) preparation; 2.) bearing away, trimming the mainsail; 3.) as main crosses, helmsman pushes tiller back toward main to check force of the crossing sail; 4.) with mainsail filled on new jibe and boat under control, helmsman steers on new course.

22. S-Jibe

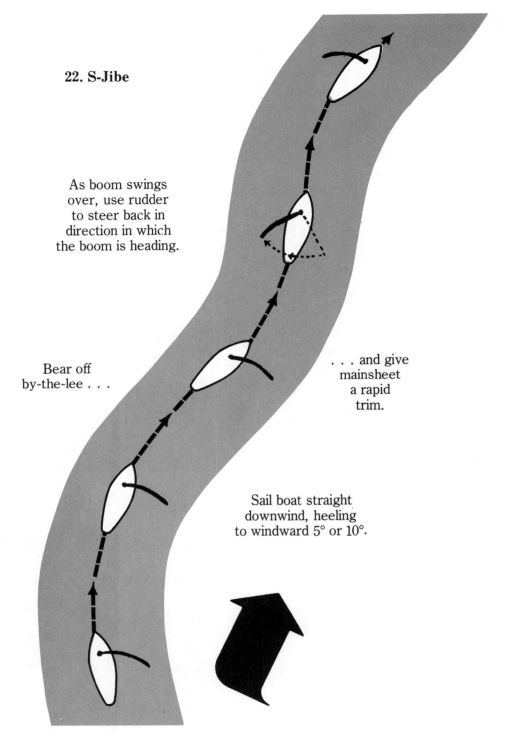

As boom swings over, use rudder to steer back in direction in which the boom is heading.

Bear off by-the-lee . . .

. . . and give mainsheet a rapid trim.

Sail boat straight downwind, heeling to windward 5° or 10°.

doesn't allow the boat to round into the wind. (Diagram 22) As the main fills on the new side, keep it overtrimmed and resume course, having completed your jibe. Don't begin to head up until the boat is under control.

The so-called "Hudson River Sloop jibe" supposedly comes from the experience of a captain sailing a sloop down the Hudson in the nineteenth century. He started a flying jibe, and the boom, some seventy feet long with a fifty-foot gaff, came crashing from one side to the other. But in coming across with so much power, the sail began to back itself and ended up floating into place on the opposite side. It's a useful way of jibing, but it doesn't work on boats with mainsail areas of less than five thousand square feet.

Sailing by-the-Lee, and Keeping the Boat Stable Downwind

Sailing by-the-lee can be an effective alternative to jibing. (Diagram 23) It works in all boats for short distances, up to ten or fifteen boat lengths, without an appreciable loss of speed. So compared with a jibe, it can gain you valuable distance to leeward. Use this maneuver when the wind is lifting you, so that it stays dead astern and you won't be sailing by-the-lee for long.

Ease out your main so that its leading edge is perpendicular to the wind. Trim the spinnaker so that as much of it as possible is exposed to the wind. Overtrim if necessary to keep the spinnaker stable. Then head the boat off by-the-lee as a wave passes underneath your stern.

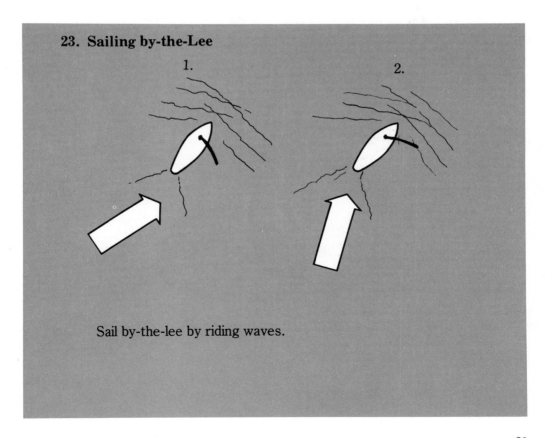

23. Sailing by-the-Lee

1.

2.

Sail by-the-lee by riding waves.

24. Downwind Stability

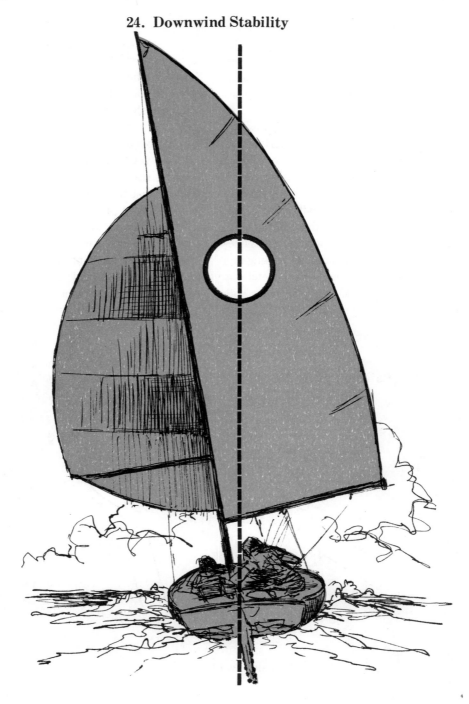

Center of effort of sails should be
directly over center of resistance of
centerboard or keel.

Keep the boomvang on relatively strong, so that the boom will not jibe. In a smaller boat, keep the centerboard down slightly, so that you don't spin out. Also, heeling the boat to windward helps you stay by-the-lee, keeping the center of effort of the sail directly over the center of resistance of the hull. Here is the key to downwind stability, whether or not you are sailing by-the-lee: the mast must be kept "over the boat," so to speak, the water pressure against the centerboard and the wind's force in the sails in balance. (Diagram 24)

If the boat is overpowered while reaching, you must return it to sailing on its lines, either by reducing sail area or by flattening out the sails. On a beam reach it is often faster to have a flat sail with more area than a full sail with less. If you cannot hold down a boat like a Laser, simply ease the boomvang off, keeping the outhaul tight. Easing the cunningham will also cause the boat to become easier to control.

Lifting up the centerboard six inches to a foot is another way to keep control of a boat that is heeling over too much. With less keel you may still have a tendency to make leeway, but not as much.

Sailing by-the-lee in a Finn, with the main eased so that it is beyond perpendicular to the mast.

Surfing, Planing, and Towing

Sailing downwind, you can gain valuable distance by getting your boat to plane, surf, surge (in the case of big boats), or catch a tow from another boat. These techniques can work well on all sailboats.

A boat planes when it breaks the water friction and rides on top of the water, sailing faster than hull speed. It surfs when it does this because of a wave. To bring the boat out of the water you must accelerate—easy enough in high winds, but difficult otherwise.

For a boat to plane, it must first of all be in balance, so that there is absolutely no pressure on the rudder. Have your sail trimmed, and keep the boat flat; a sailboat will not plane if it is heeling. As a puff hits, hike the boat down, bear off slightly, move your weight aft to get the bow to ride up over the water, and accelerate by trimming your sails rapidly. Trim your vang so that the boat is still under control but the top batten is about parallel to the boom. Ease your outhaul and cunningham, and move your jib leads outboard. Trim both the guy and the sheet of the spinnaker at the same time to increase sail area. All this will give you forward momentum to start the boat planing or surfing. Also, the centerboard should be pulled up at least halfway to reduce lateral resistance.

For surfing, the course of your boat should be perpendicular to the waves passing under your bottom. Since waves crisscross each other on diagonals, watch for them forty-five degrees on either side of your bow. Aim your bow into the deepest trough and toward the highest peak, to catch as much of the wave as possible. As the wave passes under you, give the boat some extra acceleration by trimming the sails rapidly or heeling the boat to windward

84

Top: *Mainsail turns inside out as a gust hits. Boomvang is eased to free mainsail leech.* Above: *Slack halyard and spinnaker pole set too high caused this boat to broach.* Opposite top and bottom: *420 crew trims guy and sheet for acceleration on waves.*

suddenly—in effect, rocking it. This rocking creates wind in your sails, but more important, it breaks the friction underneath the hull, so that the boat will start surfing with the wave and begin planing. Also, rapidly adjusting the helm helps to keep the boat perpendicular to the waves. Moving your weight forward will help accelerate the boat down the wave. Once you start surfing or planing, return your weight to the normal

position, and at this point keep the boat flat.

In order not to plow into the wave ahead of you once you catch a wave, bear off, staying with the wave you are on just as a surfer would—by cutting across it on a diagonal. This way you make valuable distance to leeward, staying with your puff and wave for a long time. Keep watching the waves, and practice steering from one wave to the next as long as you can. With practice

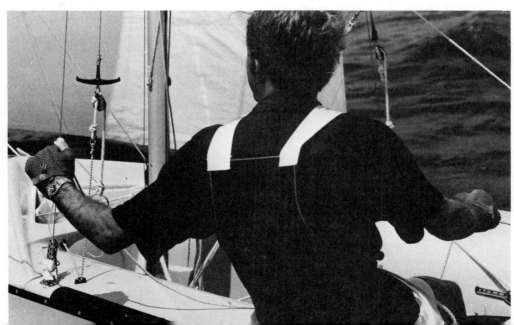

you will be able to sail fifty percent faster than the fleet every time you catch a wave, even though you are sailing by-the-lee as much as twenty or thirty degrees.

It is difficult to get larger boats to plane or surf, but you can get tremendous surges from them through a series of waves, which may lead to a surf. The problem is that the boat gets going so fast that its apparent wind dies and, without extra acceleration, cannot maintain the ride. However, boats such as Solings or larger keelboats—one-tonners, for example—do surge down waves and actually start surfing. On *Courageous* we did 14.6 knots surfing down an eight-foot wave off Breton Reef. That was our fastest. However, one-tonners can hit speeds of fifteen or sixteen knots at times while surfing.

In larger boats you can catch a tow from

1.

2.

boats bigger than yours, simply by riding their waves. It is conceivable, if the wind conditions are right, for a one-tonner to be towed across the ocean by a twelve-meter. In some races one can find as many as five boats following one another, each riding the waves of the boat ahead. Making it possible for smaller boats to sail as fast as larger ones, towing can effectively wipe out handicaps.

Towing works when the apparent wind is between 70 and 120 degrees, and when the backwind of a lead boat is not sufficient to hurt the boat behind. This is when keelboats are moving the fastest and also making the biggest waves.

To catch a tow, position your boat so that it is within one boat length astern of a boat ahead of you. This is done by heading up and going right for the stern of another boat

3.

4.

Surfing sequence (view down): 1.) with boat perpendicular to waves, skipper flattens boat and trims main; 2.) bow is pointed into trough of biggest wave; 3.) as boat starts moving down the wave, helmsman moves his weight aft to lift bow out of the water; 4.) with boat surfing, skipper moves forward, keeps boat flat, and steers with waves.

87

Boat Speed

as it passes yours—normally to windward, though preferably (for you) to leeward. (By intimidating a larger boat with a luff, you may force it to pass to leeward.) Once you are in position behind the bigger boat, your boat will be towed along at the speed of the boat ahead. (Diagram 25) The defense against a tow is to bear off sharply or come up hard, so that the boat behind has to get off the wave to avoid hitting your stern.

In a race several years ago on *Tenacious* to Key West from Fort Lauderdale, we had an all-day battle with *Running Tide*. After several hours, the twelve-meter *Heritage* came by. We were able to grab a tow from *Heritage* for about two hours, and we made up about three miles on *Running Tide* just because of it.

Practice

The best practice and experience in sailing is gained in racing, but by organizing practice sessions you will be able to concentrate on specific things without the pressure of a race. Practice sessions are easily set up, whether you practice alone, with another boat, or with a fleet. Try to practice with different sailors, so that you gain the best of what a variety of competitors can give you. Of course, you are reciprocating at the same time. Sailors are easy people to talk to, particularly after they have done well in a regatta, so spend time talking with the top finishers. You may learn something.

Opposite: *Two-tonner surfs in heavy winds off France.* Top: *Planing Dyer DT.* Above: *In the 1978 Miami-Nassau Race,* Demon *used the stern wave of* Running Tide *for a tow,* Congere *used resulting wave of both boats.*

25. Catching a Tow

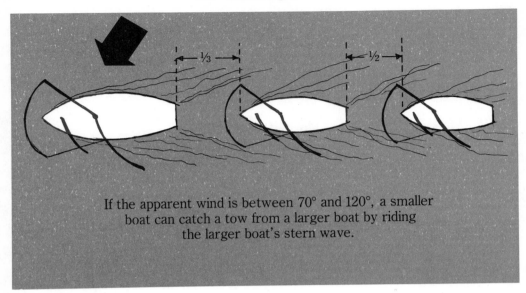

If the apparent wind is between 70° and 120°, a smaller boat can catch a tow from a larger boat by riding the larger boat's stern wave.

The boats that win in sailing are generally the fastest ones, and speed testing is the practice technique that is the key to making your boat go faster. It teaches you how to sail your boat both faster and better.

For speed testing to work properly, two boats must be set up equally and sailed in the same wind about one boat length apart—one to windward, one to leeward. Keep both boats in clear air. Each boat should be sailed as fast as possible. Then, by making one adjustment at a time and carefully observing the results as compared with the companion boat, you determine how to improve the boat's performance. If you find something that makes a boat go faster, then both boats should make that adjustment.

To keep the two boats as nearly equal as possible, switch sails back and forth. Spend time with one boat to windward and the other to leeward, and then after several minutes of sailing switch positions, so that you get the feel of both. Then, after a time, try the other tack. (Diagram 26) What you are doing is, in effect, practicing racing.

Courageous, left, *and* Independence *in their speed testing positions. Speed testing is both a gauge of a boat's speed and an excellent means of learning how to sail one's boat faster.*

26. Speed Testing

One
Boat
Length

Sail one boat length apart.
Both boats should stay in
the same wind,
keeping their own
wind clear.
Test sailing on
both tacks, swapping
windward and leeward
positions.

Communication

From the Skipper

Ted tries to break down commands in exact terms. A sail trimmer will be confused if you say something like "Ease the jib a little." What does "a little" mean: one inch? six feet? You should say, "Ease the jib three inches"; "take the halyard up one number"; "drop the traveler down two inches"; "trim in the main four inches"; and so on. Orders like these take the guesswork out of understanding the helmsman.

As for commands for a mark rounding, Ted lets the crew know that it has, say, two boat lengths to a mark, or that it will be tacking in, say, one minute. He breaks down distances into boat lengths or feet, so that everyone on board has a clear understanding of what he has to do and in what time frame.

From the Crew

Instead of pointing to a mark, tipping off other boats as to your reference point, look directly at the skipper or helmsman and tell him in a clear voice where the mark is in relation to the bow. For example, "The mark is thirty degrees off the port bow."

By using a reference point or lining up the mark with an object on shore, you make it easier to see. Batten pockets and seams in the sail make good reference points. By observing how a batten lines up with the boom, for example, you can tell whether you are properly trimmed.

The Skipper and Tactician as a Team

Every boat with more than one person sailing it should have a skipper and a tactician, capitalizing on the particular strengths of each. Collective wisdom is the key; simply, two people see more than one person does. On any watch two people should always be working together at the helm, one steering while watching the sails, angle of heel, wind, waves, and the boat in general, the other observing the competition, the boat's performance in relation to it, and new wind. By using slack periods during the race to discuss upcoming maneuvers, the skipper, tactician, and rest of the crew, if any, will be better prepared. This unusual but simple use of some free time will turn an average boat into a winner.

Part 3
On the Racecourse
tactics and strategy

Reading the Elements

Reading the elements need not be the mystery so many sailors seem to think it is. How many times have they won a beautiful start at the port end of the line, their position seemingly unbeatable, only to have the lead disappear as a major lift comes across the fleet? A bad break, of course— or was it? If all major shifts are just a matter of luck, then why do some of the top sailors continually luck out?

The key to reading the elements is trained observation. A person can actually see what the wind, current, and waves are up to. Like a golf pro studying a green before making a putt, or a surfer watching wave patterns before riding, the sailor must understand his immediate environment before deciding how to deal with it. And to do this, he must know what to look for. By following several basic rules and with continual practice, you can read the wind, current, and waves easily.

Your observation should begin before the start, while most of the fleet is relaxing. Spend this valuable time watching for patterns. By studying the elements before the start, a crew will have more time for other things during the race. Take notes every time you race. When you return to a course under similar wind conditions, you will then be a leg up on the competition. In college, Gary kept notes on two thousand races over four years. Every time he returned to a sailing site, he was better off for having detailed notes to review.

The Wind

Not all wind shifts are easy to predict, but we can aid you to see (or sense) the wind shifts before they hit.

Keep a good eye on all sources available to you. Flags, the set of marks and ships, smokestacks, race-committee pennants, the direction in which birds take off, trees, clouds, and the angle and intensity of the ripples on the water all are helpful wind indicators. (Diagram 27) Other boats are your best source, however. If possible, observe the course from a high vantage point before taking to the water. At the Timme Angsten Collegiate Regatta, held in Chicago every Thanksgiving [editor's note: won by Turner in 1959 and Jobson in 1972], one team would gain a distinct advantage by watching the wind from the top of one of the nearby apartment buildings. From there one could see clearly where the strongest wind was coming from and the time interval between puffs.

Before the start, note your compass course every few minutes. In ten to fifteen minutes, you will gain a good understanding of the wind's pattern. Often you will discover an oscillating wind shift, one in which the wind returns to within a few degrees of its original direction. By timing an oscillating shift, you will know what to expect on the windward leg. Generally, an oscillating wind will shift between five and fifteen degrees on either side of the median direction— more in an offshore breeze, because of the greater surface friction of the shore.

Wind oscillations are often consistent and therefore easy to time. The shorter the time between oscillations, the shiftier the windward leg will be. In rapidly shifting winds, it is best to go for the favored end of the starting line. If the oscillation period is long, however (equal to, say, half the time it will take to sail the windward leg), then it is important to start on the part of the line that will put you into the best po-

Opening spread: Courageous *sailing on its lines to windward in sixteen knots of breeze. Turner is at the helm.*

97

27. Wind Indicators

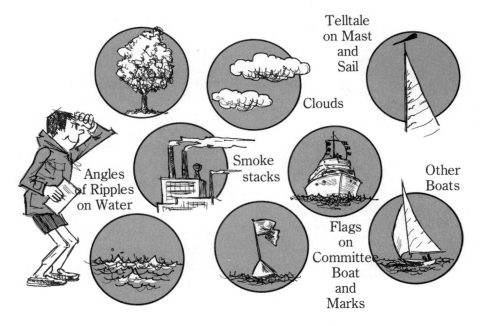

Telltale on Mast and Sail

Clouds

Angles of Ripples on Water

Smoke stacks

Other Boats

Flags on Committee Boat and Marks

sition for the first shift. For example, if the starboard end is slightly favored but you know from observation that the wind is shifting next to the left, giving a major port tack lift, it will be better to start at the port end of the line.

If the period of oscillation equals the length of time it takes to sail the windward leg, this is a "persistent shift." Here the wind does not return to its original direction for the duration of the leg. All of us have been on the outside of a persistent shift, praying for the header we know will never come. Such shifts are caused by local weather systems moving through the area, especially sea breezes, thunderstorms, and low-pressure systems.

On *Tenacious* in the 1978 Nassau Cup, we found ourselves on the wrong side of what we thought was a persistent shift. Worried about falling farther behind the leaders, we decided to bail out early and tack. Had we waited, however, we would have won the race, since the wind shifted

back to its original direction—in fact, ten degrees farther. We would have avoided this error had we timed the period of oscillation before the start. Sheer laziness did us in.

Listen to the Marine Radio or call the National Weather Service before a regatta. Their predictions are usually accurate and helpful. But do not rely on this information alone. Try to make your own predictions on the basis of experience. In addition, you might consider taking an evening course on weather or picking up a meteorology and forecasting textbook in the library.

In the Northern Hemisphere the wind tends to travel counterclockwise and inward around a low-pressure center, and the low-pressure system always moves to the east. Therefore, the wind will veer (shift to the right) when the low passes to the north of your location, and back (shift to the left) when the low passes to the south. This is most evident with the passage of a cold front, and the low preceding it, marked by an abrupt wind shift from the southwest to the northwest, along with a sudden drop in temperature.

Thunderstorms and unexpected persistent shifts often accompany cold fronts. Regardless of the original direction of the wind, you can expect a lull before the squall hits. Powerful gusts will follow from the direction of the storm, generated by heavy rain in the center of it. As the center approaches, the wind will die and the rain will get heavier.

A sea breeze arises because coastal land heats more quickly than the water. As the land heats, warm air rises from the surface, drawing in cooler air from the ocean to take the warm air's place. (Diagram 28) If the original wind is an onshore breeze, the sea breeze will reinforce it and the wind will be very strong. If the original wind is offshore, then the sea breeze will conflict with it, producing a calm spot. Calms can last just a few minutes or all day. Keep your eyes open for the new breeze. If the old breeze seems to be receding, you can bet the sea

breeze is starting to fill in. If the old breeze dies and comes back, it will be a long time until the sea breeze moves in, if it does at all.

Sea breezes often occur at the same time every day. On Long Island Sound, for example, the sea breeze is known as "the four-o'clock southerly" for its regular appearance at about that time of the afternoon.

The easiest and often most accurate method of predicting the weather is local inquiry. One morning at the 1976 Olympic Trials at Association Island, in upstate New York, Gary met an elderly lady sitting in her chair on the porch of her summer cottage. He said, "It looks like it's going to be another nice day." She replied, "Don't be so sure." She predicted thunderstorms later in the day with the wind coming right out of a clump of trees across her yard. Gary figured the direction would be about 330 degrees. About three that afternoon a thunderstorm blew over, the wind right on 330 degrees. After that incident, we talked

28. Sea Breeze

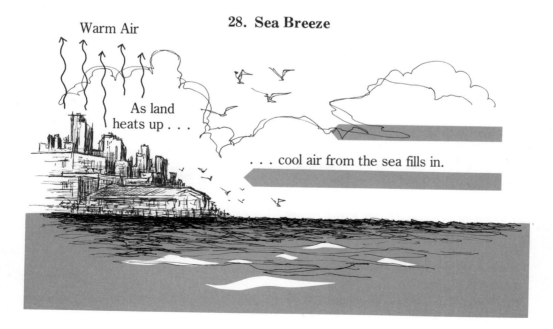

Warm Air

As land heats up . . .

. . . cool air from the sea fills in.

with that lady every morning. She had observed the weather there for many years from the same vantage point, and she knew a strong southerly would come through if there was "dew on the grass." As a rule, when in doubt talk with the locals.

A third wind-shift classification, in addition to the oscillating and persistent shifts, is the geographic shift. This is a change in wind direction or velocity caused by some obstruction, such as a hill, trees, a bank, an anchored ship, buildings, or a shoreline.

Even a spectator fleet affects the wind. We found when approaching windward marks and the finish line in the America's Cup that the wind tended to be lighter there because of all the idling yachts and ships.

The wind tends to bend around obstacles much as water tends to curve around a hull. This pattern is similar to a persistent shift. Try to sail for the center of the curve first. Be careful not to sail too close to the obstacle or you'll be blanketed by it.

In foggy conditions, the wind on the water's surface is often different from the wind aloft. Note the direction of the wind on the surface. Note the direction the clouds overhead are coming from. Generally the wind will fill in from the same direction as the clouds once the fog burns off.

Wind aloft normally changes before the wind on the surface. In boats with big rigs, watching the action of the wind at the masthead is a good guide to what the wind will do on the water.

In watching the water for wind variations, you will be more effective for a longer time if your eyes are relaxed. So use both eyes to watch the water, and don't squint. Use a fixed reference point—a sail, another boat, the mast, a landmark on shore—as a gauge. Concentrate on one section of the horizon at a time. You may miss an object or the wind's pattern if you sweep the horizon. Look for detail, allowing your eyes to focus clearly on each section of the horizon, generally thirty to sixty degrees at a time.

Check for any differences in the intensity of the ripples approaching you and the difference in the angle of these ripples. Color too is significant: darker areas generally mean more wind. Try not to second-guess what you see. Your first reaction is the best. If there looks to be more wind on one side of the course, believe it.

The leading edge of a puff of wind is normally the strongest. (Diagram 29) Don't waste the wind by tacking or jibing. Always sail into a wind shift at least two to five boat lengths before tacking. This will keep you in the new breeze longer and prevent you from tacking immediately into another header.

In small boats it is best to sail well into a puff before tacking, to maximize the strength and new direction of the wind. On larger boats, however, particularly in lighter

29. Sailing into a Header

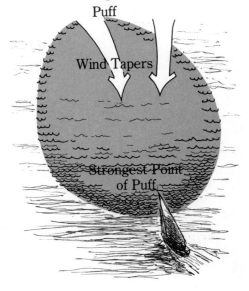

Puff

Wind Tapers

Strongest Point of Puff

winds (under five knots) that are spotty, it is often better to make your tack before a puff reaches your boat. If you wait for the puff to hit, you may use all its energy in making the tack. By setting the boat up on the desired tack just before the puff, you will be able to accelerate better as the puff hits.

If new wind is approaching from abeam, it is best to tack for it. If the wind appears to be coming from ahead, continue sailing until you are up to speed.

Be the first boat to sail for new wind. Keep a good look out for wind on the water. If you see wind, go for it.

The art of predicting wind shifts is fun. Make a habit of predicting every single puff. After a time you will develop a sixth sense about the wind, allowing you to concentrate on tactics and speed.

Waves

Waves slow your boat, especially those that are short and steep, encountered in shallow water. The best policy is to sail around them. Smoother water is found in the lee of land, ships, and jetties and in light-wind areas. Wave periods get longer as the water gets deeper.

Avoid areas where waves are landing directly against a solid surface such as a bulkhead or a jetty. The effect of the rebounding waves, resulting in very confused seas, will drastically reduce your speed. The wind tends to be confused in these areas as well.

Note while tuning up before the start whether the angle of the waves is the same on both tacks. If it is not, you will have to trim your sails differently on each tack. If you find on one tack that you are heading more directly into the waves, then you should trim for power. On the other hand, if you find on the opposite tack that you are sailing across the waves, you might want

to trim your sails so that you are pointing.

Note the direction from which the waves are hitting your boat on the windward legs. If the waves are coming from ahead, trim your jib to the outboard lead. If the waves are then approaching from abeam on the opposite tack, you may find you can point higher, without losing speed, by trimming to the inboard lead.

Waves generally have a pattern. By tuning up for at least ten to fifteen minutes before each race, you will get a feel for the waves. Observe how you are sailing compared with your competitors, and make adjustment accordingly.

The most important ingredient in sailing in waves is constant trim. Every wave changes your pitching moment and your balance. Playing your sails allows you to work through the waves. As you see a steep set of waves approaching, drive to get through them. Try to steer to avoid the worst part of the wave. If a smooth spot comes, spend the time pointing high. If you find yourself in an unusually confused area, you should look for calmer water.

Watch the action of waves about forty-five degrees on either side of your bow. (Diagram 30)

Current

Current is common to all bodies of water. It can be caused by tides, wind, rain, surges in the level of water, or even other boats. If current is uniform throughout a racecourse, it need not be considered except at the starting line or during mark roundings. However, if the current varies in velocity across a racecourse, you must plan your race carefully. Downwind, as a rule, sail against the current early in the leg, so that you will have more speed sailing with the current as you approach the next mark.

Be careful judging rhumb lines to account

30. Sailing in Waves

Head into the deepest trough,
keeping big-cresting peaks
perpendicular to your course.

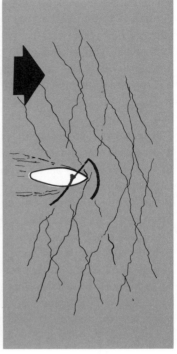

for the current. You can better determine what the current is doing by looking at lobster pots, the set of anchored vessels, or your performance compared with that of other boats. Indeed, any object in the water that is anchored to the bottom will tell you what the current is doing. The object will appear to be traveling through the water. You can judge both the direction (set) and the speed (drift) of the current by watching the water around it. A small wake will trail the object in a strong current.

Different currents in the same body of water can be detected along the line where they meet, often marked by seaweed, driftwood, or flotsam. This dividing line is known as a current sheer. Along the Gulf Stream, which travels at speeds up to four and five knots, the sheer is clearly distinguishable by contrasting water color and temperature.

After a dismal series in the 1972 Finn Olympic Trials, Gary sailed halfway up the windward leg before the last race, and at that point he found a current sheer. By throwing a life jacket on one side and luffing on the other, thereby judging the relative strengths of the two currents, he determined that the current was unfavorable on the starting-line side of the course and favorable on the windward-mark side. He started at the leeward mark and was amazed to find himself the only one sailing to the left side of the course. He even had to weave his way through the spectator fleet. When he finally tacked on the rhumb line, however, the thirty-five other Finns were abeam about one mile to leeward. He rounded the windward mark first, which made for a happy ending to a long event.

Before racing, check the Tide and Current Tables to familiarize yourself with the tidal characteristics of the area. Charts depict water depth and will indicate the kinds

A current stick is a handy device, used to detect current at a buoy. Although it may not be necessary in smooth water, it helps in large waves, where the current is difficult to judge. By means of an attached weight, a current stick stands upright in the water, sticking up several inches above the surface—high enough to be seen but low enough for the wind to have no effect on it. The current moves the stick in the direction the current is flowing. (Diagram 31)

31. Current Stick

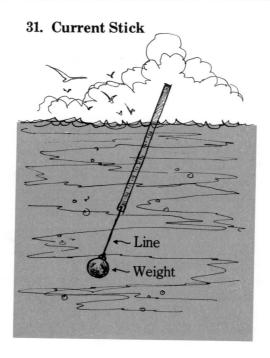

Line

Weight

of waves you might encounter. Currents are generally strongest in the deepest parts. Look for channel marks to judge currents. The effect of tide changes is felt first in shallow water. In larger bodies of water, where the tide generates momentum, the current flow is slower to change. A change in the tide can be seen from current eddies. These are normally found on the downstream side of an object jutting out into a stream—a jetty, for example.

The wind has a major effect on current. If the wind is with the current, for example, it can delay the time at which the tide changes.

Generally, one knot of current will effect the set of a ship the same as ten knots of wind. If, say, the current is two knots and the wind is blowing five knots in the opposite direction, the ship will drift with the current. On *Tenacious* during the 1977 St. Petersburg–Fort Lauderdale race, the wind died to only three knots while we were in the axis of the Gulf Stream. Yet because the current in the Stream was four knots, the apparent wind speed was seven knots. In smooth water, *Tenacious* can make five knots in that little wind. But over the bottom, we were making *nine* knots (the four knots of favorable current plus the five knots of boat speed), which is fast for three knots of true wind.

Prestart Tune-up

Before a race, many sailors will sail to windward for only a minute or two, checking lead positions and sail trim, then bear off and start maneuvering around the line. A better way of tuning is to spend at least ten minutes sailing to windward, so that you get into the groove of sailing the waves, dealing with wind shifts, and also, if you are in a small boat, hiking hard. Once you have sailed in the groove for a while, you will be prepared to pop off the starting line at the gun. Without tuning up properly, you will be slow and disorganized at the start. To get into the groove quickly, it may be helpful to use the buddy system of speed testing. (Diagram 32) Two boats start at opposite ends of the line and cross each other. After this point they sail off for two minutes, then tack simultaneously and come together again, seeing which boat gained on the other. Two more minutes of sailing away, another simultaneous tack, another coming together, and the relative positions are again noted. In this way one can determine which side of the course is favored,

32. Using the Buddy System in Tuning Up

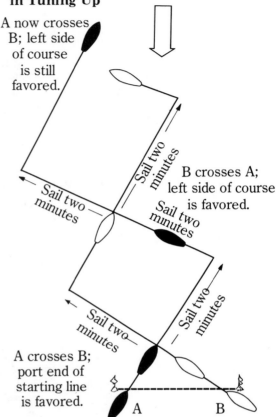

A now crosses B; left side of course is still favored.

B crosses A; left side of course is favored.

Sail two minutes

Sail two minutes

Sail two minutes

Sail two minutes

Sail two minutes

Sail two minutes

A crosses B; port end of starting line is favored.

A   B

as well as learn what adjustments one needs to make for speed. The whole process should take only about fifteen minutes.

During this tuning session, note your compass courses so as to get an idea of what the wind is doing. An anemometer reading tells you how strong the wind is, allowing you to make the best sail selection. It is absolutely critical to have the right sail up as you come off the starting line.

It is important in trial runs to determine your bearings when you are on the starting line, so that you will know at the actual start when you are on the line. (Diagram 33)

Sight down through the starting line and line up one end of the line with an object on shore. As you approach the line for the

33. The Starting Line

Sight down the line to get a bearing.

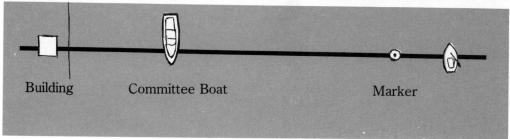

Building   Committee Boat   Marker

start, you will know how that marker lines up with the starting line and, hence, just when you'll be on the line. The crew should stay low, so that the helmsman, tactician, and bowman can see, and no one but they should talk. Work out a system of hand signals for the bowman to signal the cockpit when to go for the line, bear off, slow down, speed up, or duck behind a boat if you are overlapped. Only the helmsman of your boat should hail other boats; random hails from crew members show a poorly organized ship.

Starting Techniques

Winning a start gives you a psychological lift that makes you and your crew work harder for the rest of the race. And it enables you to look around and pick the best time to tack.

The first problem on the starting line is choosing at which end to start. Traditionally, most sailors will luff in the middle of the line, noting which end of the line seems closer to the bow as they luff up. (Diagram 34) Although this technique is common, and works, it does not allow for current and direction of waves. The best method we know of in starting is to sail across the line at one end while another boat is crossing the line at the opposite end. By noting which boat crosses the other's path first, you can determine which end of the line is favored. (Diagram 35)

The key to any start is setting yourself in position so that you will have speed coming off the line. The trick here is to maneuver with speed during the starting sequence. The faster your boat is moving, the

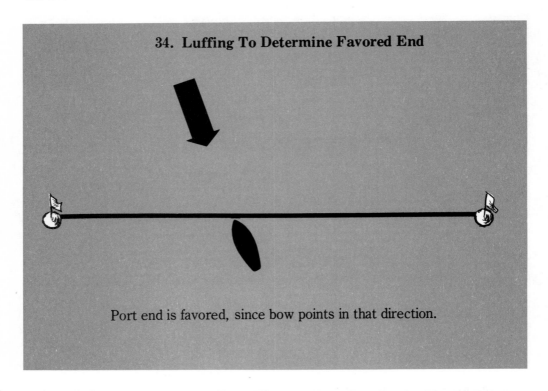

34. Luffing To Determine Favored End

Port end is favored, since bow points in that direction.

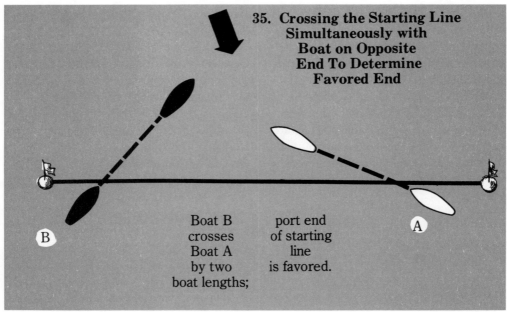

35. Crossing the Starting Line Simultaneously with Boat on Opposite End To Determine Favored End

Boat B crosses Boat A by two boat lengths; port end of starting line is favored.

easier it is to maneuver around other boats. Amazingly, most sailors start by sitting on the line luffing, waiting for the gun to go off and then trimming in at the starting signal. Or they simply reach down the line and head up at the gun. Both these tactics are inadequate. Consider for a minute two race-car drivers in their cars. The first is sitting on the starting line revving his engine. When the flag goes down, he puts the pedal to the floor and takes off. The second driver has started his car already and when the flag goes down will hit the line at ninety miles per hour. It's obvious which has the advantage. The same idea applies to sailing.

On *Courageous* in 1977, we tried having both the helmsman and the tactician call starts. We found the helmsman to be the better person, because he has a better view of the overall situation and a better sense of how the boat is responding as it accelerates, particularly in relation to the rest of the fleet. A second person, the tactician, can be helpful by letting the helmsman know how far in distance and time the boat is from

the line, how it stands in relation to other boats, where it is in relation to the lay lines, and how much time is left to the starting gun.

There is really no magic to winning a start. The trick is getting away from the starting line consistently with clear air and speed, so that you pop out ahead of the rest of the fleet. Even if you are sailing a slow boat, you can make consistently good starts if, through practice, you master one of several starting techniques.

The Timed Run

Properly executed, a timed run (also known as the Vanderbilt start) brings you to the starting line with speed as the race begins. It works well because a sailboat goes the same speed close-hauled as it does on a broad reach. Therefore, if you run away from the line for one minute, it will take you one minute to return (not counting the maneuvering to head back). As a rule, we recommend that you set your timed run so that you are maneuvering when no one else is.

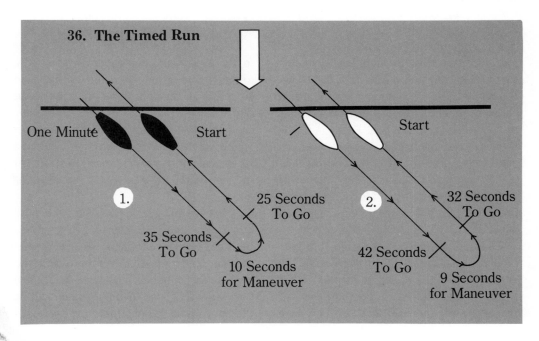

36. The Timed Run

One Minute   Start

1.

25 Seconds To Go

35 Seconds To Go

10 Seconds for Maneuver

Start

2.

32 Seconds To Go

42 Seconds To Go

9 Seconds for Maneuver

Instead of the standard two- or four-minute timed run, try one of a minute and thirty-five seconds, or two minutes and fifteen seconds. (Diagram 36) If you still encounter congestion, such as a "stack" of boats, do not take any unnecessary risks by starting in their vicinity. You might decide to start just to leeward of the stack, where you will be assured of clear air.

The timed run is most effective on the windward part of the starting line.

Our experience shows that the timed run works best on bigger yachts. It also works well in dinghies, but when the ends are crowded it is difficult to get clear air. On keelboats, ranging from Shields and Solings up to twelve-meters, the timed run works well because it takes a long time for these boats to build up speed, so the momentum of a properly executed timed run is a great advantage. For the same reason, the timed run works well on a downwind start.

Every five or ten seconds during the starting sequence, the crew should call the minutes and seconds remaining until the starting gun. Speak directly to the skipper, in a normal tone of voice.

If your competitors are barging down on you, hail a warning to them early, so that there can be no confusing your right of way. Do not wait for the gun to go off and a collision to occur before you state your rights. Anticipate. If a boat looks as if it is about to tack under your lee bow, you can discourage this by heading right at that boat and forcing it to tack away early or, better yet, to sail past you and tack later. Under the rules there is no proper course before the start, so you may maneuver at will.

The trick to starting is to keep your boat moving, reaching as much as possible, so that you have the speed in relation to the other boats to be able to pop into clear air when you hit the line. If there is a boat ahead of you as you approach the line and you have the option to pass to leeward or to windward, do not pass to leeward unless you are absolutely certain of breaking through. If, for example, the boat ahead is moving at two-thirds speed with sails full, it is better to pass to windward. If the boat ahead is parked and stopped with both sails luffing, then passing to leeward can work.

The Port Approach

The port approach is a popular starting technique because it is easy to work, particularly at the leeward end of the line. You sail "against the grain," approaching the fleet on port tack, and tack into a hole that you find on the line. Once again, the trick is to keep your boat moving at maximum speed, allowing you to make a smooth tack into position. (Diagram 37) When you make your tack for the line, it is important not to tack too close to a leeward boat. Try to make your tack at least two to three boat lengths to windward of him. (Diagram 38)

The port approach is actually a timed run in which you are moving close-hauled and at full speed in the last thirty seconds so as to hit the line and pop ahead. A good way to find a hole is to look for boats that have been luffing for some time—say, between thirty seconds and one minute. These are the boats that will not be able to maneuver when you tack underneath them. You must be careful on the port approach to stay clear of the starboard-tack boats approaching you.

If you are going for a port-end start, note how much time you have as you approach the fleet on port and pass the port end of the line. (Diagram 39) If half the time to the start goes by before you tack, you know that you will be able to tack, trim in, and hit the buoy at full speed. However, if you see

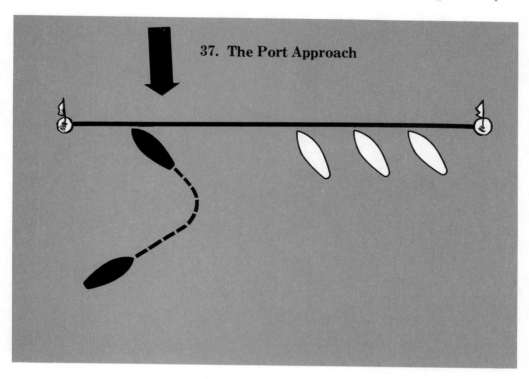

37. The Port Approach

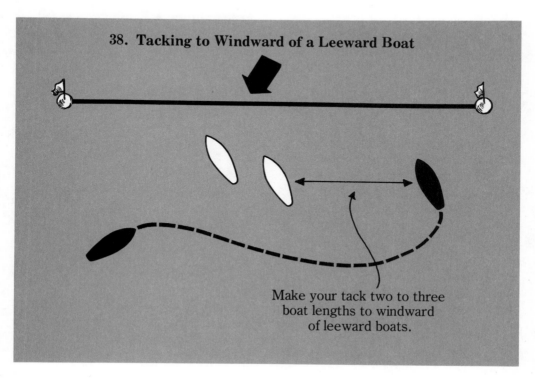

38. Tacking to Windward of a Leeward Boat

Make your tack two to three
boat lengths to windward
of leeward boats.

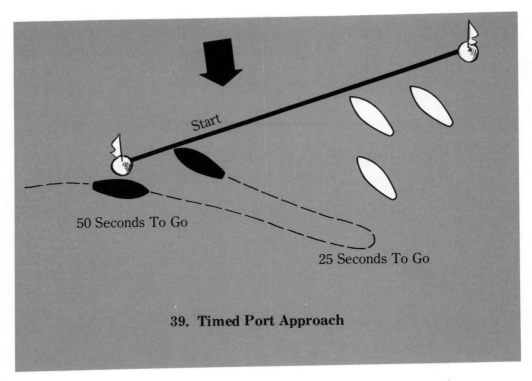

39. Timed Port Approach

seven or eight boats that are about to get hung up on the mark, sail to windward of the stack before making your final approach to the line on starboard.

The Dip Start

The dip start works well in planing dinghies, particularly when a strong current is running down or through the line or when it is difficult to cross the line on starboard tack. The following dip start works best in the middle of the line: Simply sit about five to ten boat lengths to windward of the line, observing where holes develop in the fleet. Approach the line on a *broad* reach, and head up to a close-hauled course about twenty seconds before the gun goes off. (Diagram 40) If a leeward boat is preventing you from getting back to the line (Diagram 41), jibe to port, sailing astern of that boat, before making your dip.

As you make your dip, round the boat

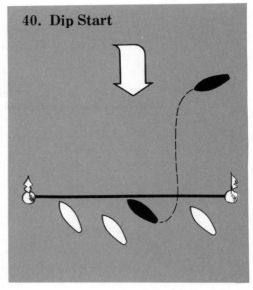

40. Dip Start

up, keeping the boat as flat as possible to prevent making leeway. Trim your sails as you round up, moving the tiller slowly, so that you do not lose speed. The faster you

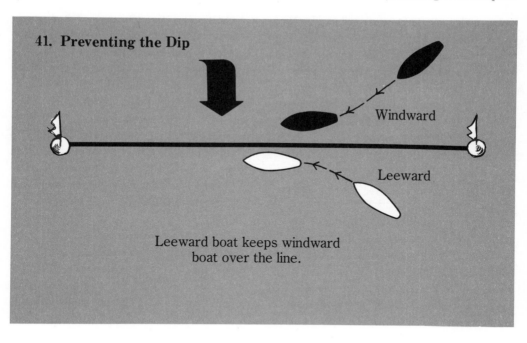

41. Preventing the Dip

Windward

Leeward

Leeward boat keeps windward
boat over the line.

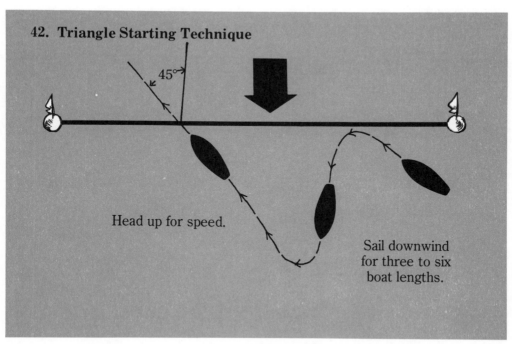

42. Triangle Starting Technique

45°

Head up for speed.

Sail downwind
for three to six
boat lengths.

spin a sailboat, the faster it will slow down; if you want to maintain your speed, make your rounding slowly. The General Recall rule, which prohibits boats from being over the starting line within one minute of the gun, has severely restricted the dip start. But it is still a successful technique in fast, maneuverable boats and in small fleets which allow enough room for the maneuver.

The Triangle Starting Techniques

There are two triangular methods of starting that we find effective. In the first, which works well in a dinghy, you pick a point on a starting line and sail directly downwind, harden up, and approach the line at full speed. (Diagram 42) This clears out a space on the starting line. Peter Commette used this start successfully in qualifying for the 1976 Olympics in Finns.

The second triangular approach is simply starting on the line, sailing downwind, jibing onto port, and sailing abeam of the line before tacking over to starboard in making your approach. (Diagram 43) This technique is a modified port approach that helps you start at a particular point on the line while clearing a zone for you to sail into when you make your final approach. Once again, with both these techniques it is imperative to be moving close-hauled and at full speed on starboard tack when the gun goes off.

Check the wind direction and your compass on every tack before the start. This keeps you up on any changes in the wind and confirms which end of the line is favored. If you find that one end of the line is no longer favored, bail out and go for the other end. The trick is to keep your eyes open all the time.

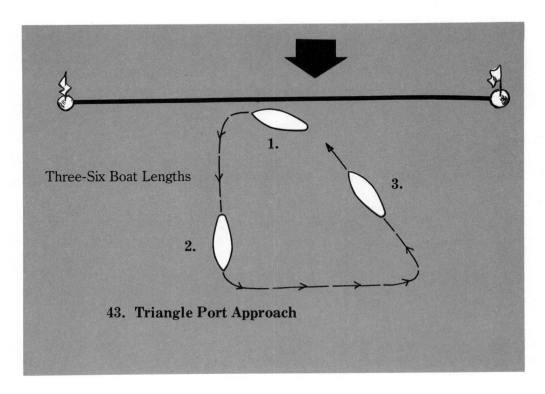

Three-Six Boat Lengths

1.

2.

3.

43. Triangle Port Approach

If you find that you are going to be over the line or are going to run into a buoy, the time to bail out is early. Do not wait until the starting gun to correct your error. If you are going to be early, slow down in plenty of time, so that on your final approach to the line you are accelerating again. Do not let your boat be one that is slowing down at the start. You'll be losing maneuverability as you lose momentum.

To avoid collisions, keep a good lookout when sailing around. Concentrate hard on your start. Do not sail around wishing everyone good luck; nice guys like that finish last. The time to be aggressive at the start is when the warning signal goes off. If you see a difficult situation developing with another boat, hail your intentions early, so that there is no misunderstanding. If you find yourself being tailed, shake off the other boat early, so that you do not end up in trouble. It is imperative to protect your leeward bow on the starting line; do not allow boats to tack to leeward of you. Keep your options open during the starting sequence and do not commit yourself to one end of the line or the other until you are absolutely sure which is better. If you think that one end is favored and all the other boats are at the wrong end, be a little bit sneaky and wait until the last minute to sail down to the favored end, so that no other boat follows you there. If you know that you can get away with a port-tack start, do not cross the line six or seven times on port tack and give away the secret. Wait until the gun goes off to reveal it.

By understanding these starting techniques, you will know in a short time which boats are making good approaches to the line and which boats will have trouble. It is always a good idea to start near boats you think will be slow coming off the line, to help you pop out into that valuable lead. By using one of these starting techniques and keeping these pointers in mind, in a short time you will be able to start consistently with clear air and speed and as a result dramatically improve your racing.

Starting Techniques in Large Fleets

We have found in recent years that on crowded starboard-tack lines, particularly in the Finn and Laser classes, three or four rows of boats will stack up gunwale to gunwale on the line. Sometimes they are as much as two to three minutes early, making the start impossible. In this case, the answer is "If you can't beat 'em, join 'em." Several rules of thumb to follow:
1. When you are luffing on the line, never let your boat go slower than your competition. During one America's Cup starting sequence, it looked to most of the spectators as if *Courageous* were sitting luffing, but we were actually sailing at a speed of about four and a half knots. Anytime we found ourselves slower than that we accelerated, so that we could still maneuver easily. In a dinghy, keep the boat moving as you approach the line. Keep your boat on the course that you will be sailing after the start, so that you will not have to bear off to accelerate. In a dinghy it helps to keep your boat heeled slightly to leeward. As you trim your sails, and flatten out the boat, you create wind in your sails, which gives you quick acceleration. If a boat is heeling to windward, it sideslips, and you have to bear off and heel the boat to leeward before you can begin making headway.

Always fight to be in that first group of boats; you can do it by crabbing to windward. (Diagram 44) Crabbing is simply that technique whereby at half speed, you continually luff into the wind, taking bites to

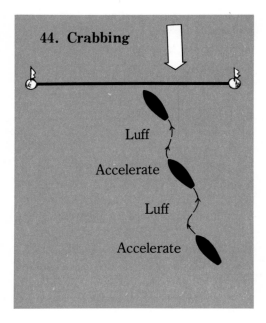

44. Crabbing

Luff

Accelerate

Luff

Accelerate

windward to stay away from the boats to leeward of you.

In large, aggressive fleets, competitors sit on the line luffing as early as two or three minutes before the starting gun, and the result is many general recalls. Most race committees would do well to institute a five-minute rule in such circumstances, automatically disqualifying any boat that is over the line within five minutes before the start, even if there is a general recall.

Dealing tactically with large, aggressive fleets is a difficult but not impossible problem. The best spots on the line, other than the pole position, which only one or two boats will be able to attain, are found either just to windward or just to leeward of a stack of boats.

Stacks more commonly form to leeward. The standard routine is for a boat to luff on the line and a second boat to sail to leeward of it, then to luff up underneath it. The process is repeated until a stack of ten or more boats is formed on the line (or, probably, over it), all madly trying to avoid collision

Jobson, Sam Merrick, and Stretch Ryder effect leeward-end start in the Soling Bowl, Annapolis.

with one another. Parked boats tend to act as magnets.

The best solution to these stacks seems to be to approach them on port tack, sailing against the grain. This way, holes in the line are easy to find. The key here is to pick just where to make your move to the line, tacking onto starboard. If the stacks are forming to leeward, this means the stack (the number of boats end to end on one another's sterns) is shallow. Therefore, you should have room to sail all the way to the windward side of the stack. After sailing at least two or three boat lengths past the windward boat in the stack, tack onto starboard and accelerate.

If the stack is deep (many boats end to end on one another's transoms), then it is best to tack to leeward and ahead of the stack. You simply will not have the room to sail through the congestion.

Coming off the Line

A good start puts you into position to move ahead of the fleet. Then you must take advantage of that position. At this point, immediately after the gun, the object is simple speed. If necessary, you can drive off a few degrees to go faster than your competition. But if there are boats on your leeward quarter, fight to stay high, so that you will not fall down into them.

The first start in every series is the most exciting. Coming off the starting line in the America's Cup races, all of us on *Courageous* felt we were slightly slower than the Australians, but as we settled down we

Laser 63624 has chosen a good time to tack to port, using boats to leeward as blockers.

eventually worked out a two-boat-length lead. Had our crew been a little calmer, we probably would have gained our lead sooner than we did. Do not be concerned with unraveling sheets or calming the crew. Concentrate on speed.

If you find you are not moving fast enough right after the start, your first reaction should be to ease your sails to gain speed. Ease the cunningham or halyards, move the jib leads forward, or drop the traveler. In college racing it helps simply to bear off a little bit. You lose valuable distance to the leaders if you concentrate only on slowing down boats around you. If there is a boat to leeward of you, bear off and drive over it, easing your sails to capture that boat's wind and forcing it to tack away. If there is a boat to windward of you, use it as a benchmark as to how high you are pointing, but do not pinch and slow down.

Observe which side of the fleet seems to be doing better after the start. This will give an early indication of which side of the course is favored and where the first shift is going to be.

In this early part of the race it is critical to keep your air clear. You can tell if your air is being blanketed by observing the speed of the boats around you and their wind pennants. If a boat to windward has its masthead fly pointing in your direction, that boat is probably hurting your wind. It is amazing how far wind shadows are projected. In many boats the wind shadow extends between four and six mast lengths. If you are in this zone, you can be assured that you are being blanketed. Also, there is a zone of backwind that extends about four to six mast lengths to windward and behind a leeward boat. (Diagram 45) If you are in this zone, you are being hurt too, though not as badly as if you are blanketed. You can sail effectively in another boat's bad

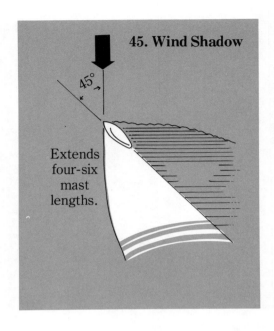

45. Wind Shadow

Extends four-six mast lengths.

air for long periods of time, losing only one or two boat lengths. And sailing in backwind is generally better than being forced to tack with no speed into a fleet of oncoming starboard-tack boats.

Sailors who are slow coming off the starting line commonly err by making too many tacks. If for any reason you find yourself behind after the start, having missed a shift, having been at the wrong end of the line, or just having had a bad start, do not tack blindly to get clear air. Tack to clear your wind only if you can be sure of staying in clear air for a long time. A sailboat loses about one to two and a half boat lengths tacking and trying to regain its speed. On *Courageous* we lost as many as three lengths. If you make three tacks after starting and the competition does not tack at all, you may lose up to seven or eight boat lengths. Moreover, you'll be unlikely to regain this distance, since usually you'll be forced to sail in bad air. So set up for one key tack after the start.

We suggest using a lead-boat strategy.

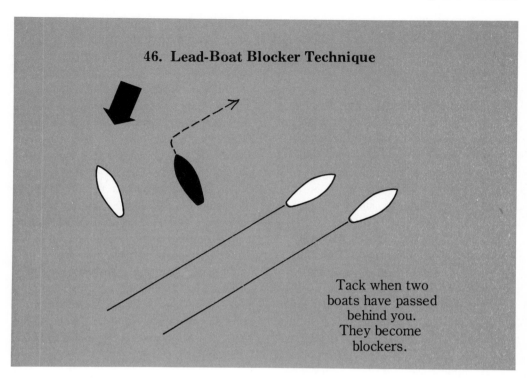

46. Lead-Boat Blocker Technique

Tack when two
boats have passed
behind you.
They become
blockers.

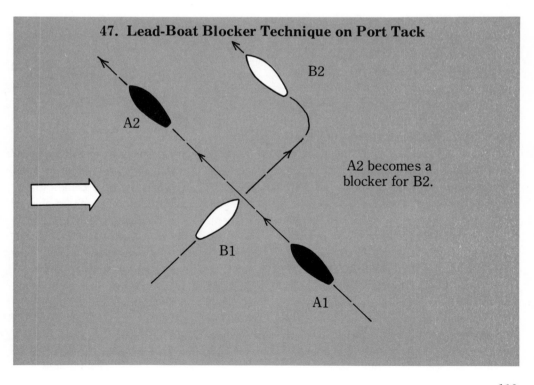

47. Lead-Boat Blocker Technique on Port Tack

B2

A2

A2 becomes a
blocker for B2.

B1

A1

Just as in football a runner uses blockers to clear his path, in sailing you can use one or two boats as "blockers" to clear a path for you. Wait until at least one or two boats have tacked to port, have sailed behind you, and are a good five to ten boat lengths to windward of your wake. Make your tack at this point, using these boats as blockers. (Diagram 46) Your lee bow is now shielded from boats that might backwind you, and you are free to sail in clear air. This tactic is very effective on all kinds of boats in short races.

The lead-boat technique works well on port as well as starboard tack. (Diagram 47) As a lead boat sails across oncoming starboard-tack boats, it clears a shield zone by blanketing the boats it crosses. Not wanting to be tacked on, a starboard-tack boat may waive her right to the rule and dip the port-tack boat. The port-tack lead boat may tack on the approaching starboard-tack boat, slowing down both boats and allowing you to gain distance. Two blockers are even more effective.

Generally, you should tack when headed. Sail into the header at least two boat lengths before you tack, so that you sail on the new lift longer. (Diagram 48) You may also tack to avoid especially bad waves. Keep a good watch out for oncoming waves. As boating gets more popular, we are finding more and more powerboats plying our waters on the weekends. If you see a bad set of waves coming, it may be advantageous to tack so that you sail parallel to the waves, keeping up your speed. Other times, you may tack to ride them. On many boats Gary has sailed, particularly the Finn and the Flying Dutchman, it is best to ride the waves. You can actually sail on a plane upwind by riding waves if you catch them just right. When you do tack, look for a soft spot on the waves when you are at maximum speed, so

that in coming off a wave you do not pound down and reduce your speed.

If you have to tack to give room to a right-of-way boat or an obstruction, be careful not to put yourself in a worse position. If, for example, you are coming off the leeward end of the line and the entire fleet tacks, it is up to you to tack and cover them. However, where the competition goes is only a reference for what you should do. It is more important to stay in phase ("phasing") with the wind shifts early in a race and in subsequent windward legs than to tack on the competition. If you single out a particular boat and tack on that boat several times, often that sailor will come back to haunt you by tacking on your wind later in the race. Try to look at the fleet as objects and as a measure of how well you are doing on the windward leg, not as individuals you have to beat.

Windward Tactics

Try to plan your crossing and maneuvering systems in advance, while sailing in open water. Then, when the time comes to implement your strategy, you will be able to concentrate on handling and speed. In a boat as simple to sail as a Laser, you can spend about eighty percent of your time thinking of tactics and looking around. In a boat like a twelve-meter, one person has to worry about steering while another concentrates on tactics. On *Courageous* we developed a general game plan before each race and then it was up to the tactician to

48. Tacking When Headed

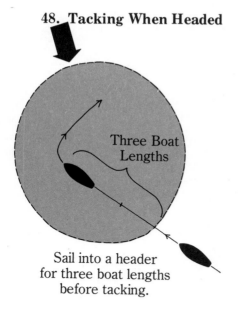

Three Boat Lengths

Sail into a header
for three boat lengths
before tacking.

49. Tacking Upwind of Opposing Boat (I)

When the masthead fly points at leeward boat, leeward boat is being hurt the most.

get the twelve-meter to follow the plan.

We learned early in the *Courageous* campaign how important it is for the tactician and helmsman to work as a unit. This kind of sailing applies to all sailboats. It's quite simple: the crew as well as the skipper must be attuned to tactics, wind shifts, and the rules, because the crew as well as the skipper handles the boat.

Using a starboard-tack advantage is your most aggressive tactic on the windward leg. Using your wind to blanket the wind of opponents is also effective. These two tactics, along with using other boats as blockers, will help keep your wind clear throughout the windward leg.

Keep Rule 41 in mind: A yacht that is either tacking or jibing shall keep clear of a yacht on a tack; furthermore, a yacht that either tacks or jibes has the onus of satisfying the race committee that she has completed her tack or jibe clear of other boats.

There are four ways to tack on another boat. First and most effective is to tack directly upwind of it. (Diagram 49) Notice

where the masthead fly or telltales are flowing, so you can recognize where the apparent wind is. Cross the boat by at least one and a half boat lengths and end up both ahead and to windward, thereby slowing down your opponent and forcing him to tack away. (Diagram 50)

The second method is to tack directly in front, taking care not to tack too close. Tacking in front of a boat has a damaging psychological as well as tactical effect on the opposition. You should cross about one and a half boat lengths in front of the other boat, so that you can complete your tack at least one boat length ahead of it and there can be no question that you made a proper tack. (Diagram 51) As a general rule, allow between one and three boat lengths of lost distance for a tack.

The third blanketing tack is to make a safe leeward tack underneath the other boat, instead of barely crossing it. Your stern should be even with the mast or bow of the windward boat when you complete your tack. If you can accomplish this, the

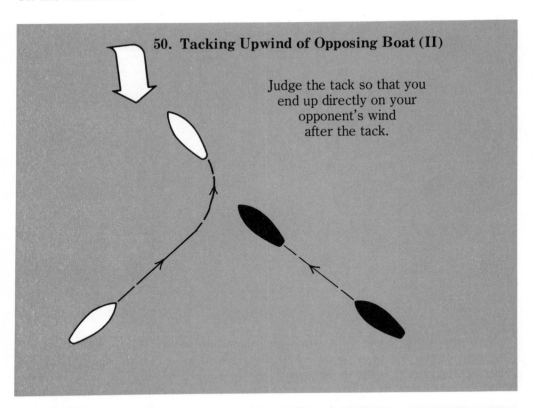

50. Tacking Upwind of Opposing Boat (II)

Judge the tack so that you
end up directly on your
opponent's wind
after the tack.

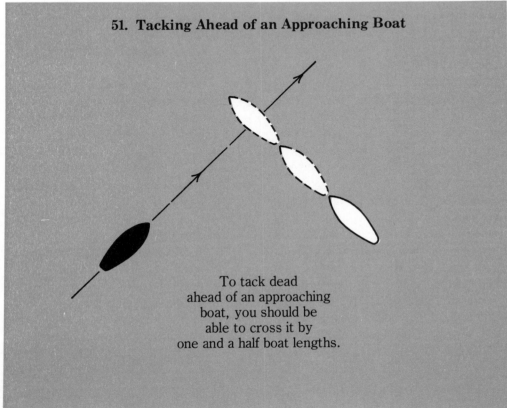

51. Tacking Ahead of an Approaching Boat

To tack dead
ahead of an approaching
boat, you should be
able to cross it by
one and a half boat lengths.

52. Covering from Behind

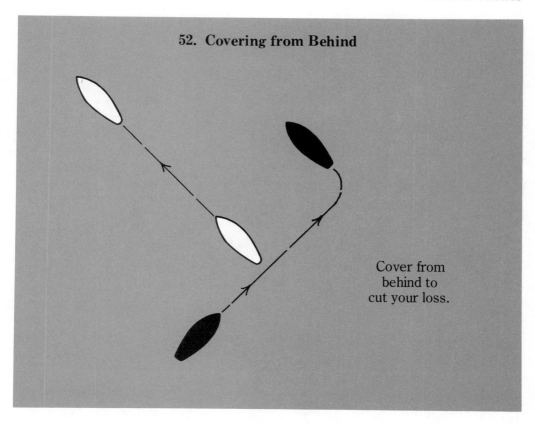

Cover from
behind to
cut your loss.

other boat will be forced to tack away.

The fourth method of tacking is covering from behind (Diagram 52), when, for example, in a match race you do not want the boat ahead to get too far away. To accomplish this, sail about five or six boat lengths past the wake of the boat ahead of you and then tack. If the other boat does not tack on you immediately, it will lose appreciable distance, because it will have to make two tacks to get back to cover you. You will cut the lead of the opposition substantially if both boats are lifted.

Under the rules, if two boats are tacking simultaneously, "the one on the other's port side shall stay clear." However, when two boats are tacking and you are the boat that is going to be to leeward after the tack, you should make your tack slowly to force the boat that is going to be windward into your backwind. (Diagram 53) If you are to leeward and ahead and are tacking simultaneously with another boat that is going to be to leeward of you, make your tack slowly, so that you end up with clear air.

Always remember: Don't tack unless you are sailing at full speed.

As you work your way up the windward leg, watch what the wind is doing, so that you can anticipate how hard to hike, how much to bear off, or how much to head up. We work the boat through the wind in strict accordance with what is happening at the moment, constantly adjusting the trim of our sails. We think that playing our sails was one of our strongest assets when we sailed *Tenacious* and *Courageous*. This "shifting gears," as some sailors call it,

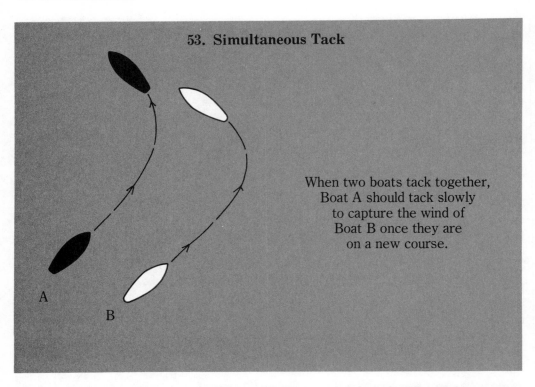

53. Simultaneous Tack

When two boats tack together,
Boat A should tack slowly
to capture the wind of
Boat B once they are
on a new course.

A

B

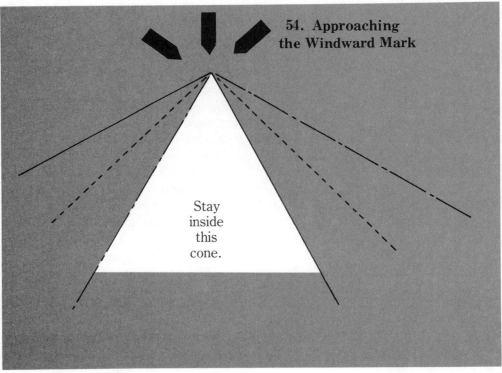

54. Approaching
the Windward Mark

Stay
inside
this
cone.

must be done constantly to get the boat through the wind as easily as possible. With every puff you play your sails and adjust your weight. In some boats, you must move carefully in order not to slow the boat down. However, in dinghies like Lasers you almost have to bang the boat around to get as much speed out of it as you can.

When sailing on the windward leg, watch your competitors and try to stay between them and the wind, keeping in mind where the mark and the lay lines are, so that you do not overshoot the mark. (Diagram 54) If a majority of the fleet is getting to the left of you, this might be an indication that you should be sailing with them to protect yourself against a backing shift. On the other hand, if the boats are getting to your right, you should protect the right side.

By staying with the fleet, you will be assured of staying close to the leaders and not ending up hopelessly behind. Sailors who go for big leads in races sometimes attain those leads but more often than not end up losing big. The trick to winning in sailing is being consistent and playing the percentages. When you want to hurt your competitors, tack on them and force them to tack. However, if you want the competition to sail nearby, let them have clear air.

If you are a right-of-way boat, try to sail right up to the burdened boat and force it to change course. (Diagram 55) A common error, we find, is for a starboard tacker to let a port tacker off the hook by tacking several boat lengths away. Both boats are now on port tack, and the boat to leeward has given away her starboard advantage. Sail right up to boats and force them to dip you or to tack away before you make your move. You want to slow down your competition when you have the opportunity, without slowing down your own boat.

If you are well downwind of the windward

55. Using the Starboard-Tack Advantage

When you have the right of way, make burden boats maneuver around you.

mark and there is plenty of time to sail to either side of the course, this is the time to make your competition maneuver around you.

This technique works particularly well in heavier boats—keelboats, ocean racers—but can be worked effectively in dinghies too. Without losing speed, you head up into the wind to gain windward distance and at the same time hurt a competitor's wind. (Diagram 56) When you are close-hauled at full speed, pick a time when you are sailing in

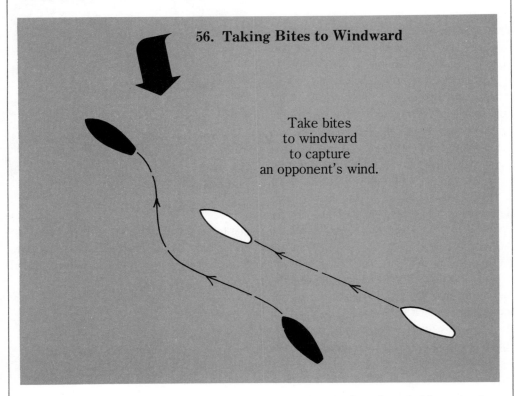

56. Taking Bites to Windward

Take bites
to windward
to capture
an opponent's wind.

relatively flat water or smooth waves and head the boat up into the wind between two and five degrees. When making this alteration of course, keep the boat flat and trim your sails as you head up, rounding your boat into the wind. This technique is called steering with your sails. Keep the boat on the new course for one to three boat lengths until you just begin to slow down. Then, never allowing your boat to go slower than your competitor's, head back down to your original course.

Taking a bite to windward is an effective way of hurting the air of a windward boat. The trick is to have full speed while keeping the boat flat and continually trimming sails. The heavier the boat, the bigger the bite you can take. On *Courageous* we were able to alter our course from three to ten degrees without losing more than one-tenth of a knot in speed. We would work our way up the windward leg scalloping about a half to one and a half boat lengths at a bite, every two minutes.

The leeward boat has the advantage, since it picks the time it wants to "take a bite." If the leeward boat loses too much speed, however, the windward boat may be able to drive over and take the leeward boat's wind. (Diagram 57)

When sailing as the windward boat, you may be in a position to "take a dive" to capture your opponent's wind. This is bearing off to gain speed and to hurt the wind of the leeward boat. Once again, it is important to keep the boat flat when taking a dive. Prepare for this by dropping your traveler and easing the sheets, or by moving

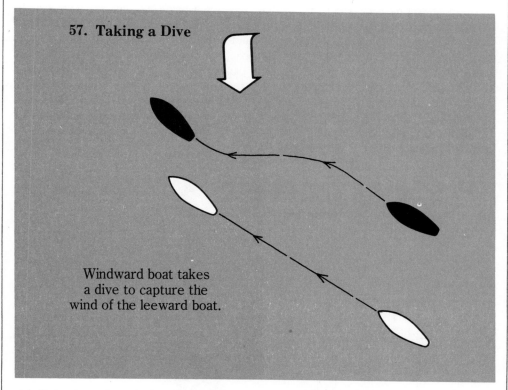

57. Taking a Dive

Windward boat takes
a dive to capture the
wind of the leeward boat.

the jib leads outboard. A sailboat will increase speed only when the sails have been eased.

Try to "dive" when the boat to leeward has slowed down after a bite and you are confident that you will not fall into its bad air. The boat that does the better job of "diving" or "biting" will establish the lead and either force the other boat away or take its air. This, incidentally, is the real war of twelve-meter sailing and can be the real war of any two well-sailed boats.

Dipping

When on port tack dipping a starboard tacker, keep your boat flat. When you make your dip, begin dipping early, but head directly at the helmsman of the other boat to discourage him from tacking on your wind. As you pass behind the other boat, your boat should already be sailing to windward and can actually get a small lift off the main of the boat you have dipped. (Diagram 58) When you begin the dip, use your sails to accelerate, and trim them to help you round up, so that you do not have to use much tiller. The bigger your boat, the tougher it is to make a good dip. By making a dip in this manner, you will lose very little distance. If you are dipping a starboard tacker, you want to discourage the other boat from tacking on you. You have the right, under the racing rules, to tack simultaneously with the boat on your port side—the starboard tacker—and it must stay clear. So a good defense against a tack here is to tack simultaneously with the tacking boat you have just dipped. This keeps him from tacking on your air. You can also intimidate an opponent by giving a hail not to tack too close and by heading right at the other boat.

58. Dipping

If you feel that you are sailing into a header, foot to the new header early, for speed. On the other hand, if you feel the wind is going to lift on the course, try to position your boat so that you are on the inside of the lift. (Diagram 59) This may mean tacking on the lift, if the lift is just beginning. The danger here is being caught "sailing around the world"—being continually lifted around the windward mark. The way out of this trap is to tack at the first indication of a new lift to get on the inside of the circle.

When behind, do not be overly concerned with other boats around you. Since you, as well as the boats around you, are already behind the leader, none of you has much to gain from jousting with another. All of you have to make up distance, and the way to do it is to concentrate on speed and on gain-

ing the next wind shift. Generally, the longer the race goes, the farther back the boats in the pack get. The rich get richer, the poor poorer. Nevertheless, in the early part of the race you still have the opportunity to get back close to the leader. It is important to stay in phase with wind shifts. At times, particularly in shifty air, it is better to sail on a lift and be in another boat's blanketing zone than to continually sail off on a header just to keep your wind clear. Most importantly, don't get depressed when you are behind. Take the attitude that you are sailing to enjoy yourself. See how well you can do just for fun in the rest of the race. In this manner you will be starting to concentrate instead of needlessly worrying about why you are at the back of the fleet. Being behind happens to all of us, but the best sailors can work themselves out of the

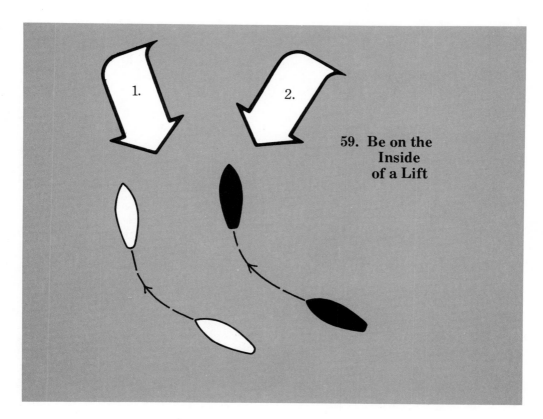

59. Be on the
Inside
of a Lift

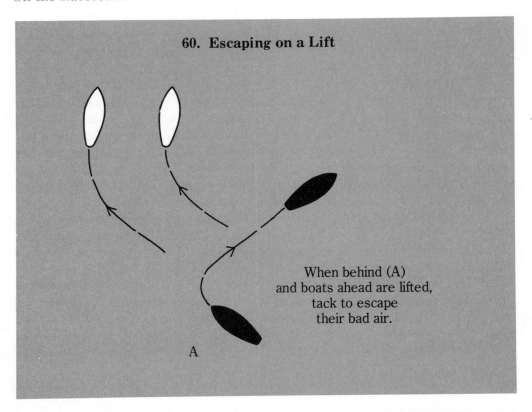

60. Escaping on a Lift

When behind (A)
and boats ahead are lifted,
tack to escape
their bad air.

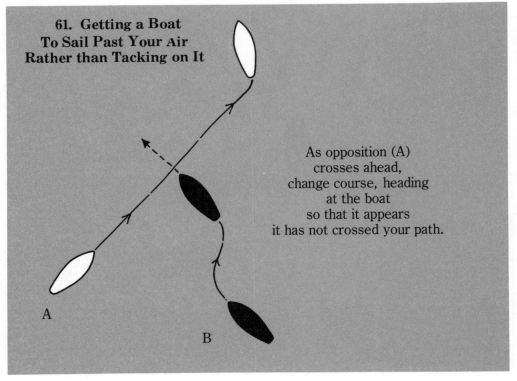

61. Getting a Boat To Sail Past Your Air Rather than Tacking on It

As opposition (A)
crosses ahead,
change course, heading
at the boat
so that it appears
it has not crossed your path.

hole by relaxing and concentrating intently.

If you are to leeward and behind several boats, you can use the wind shifts to escape from their bad air. For example, if you and the boats ahead of you as well are getting a slight lift (Diagram 60), this is a good time to tack away to escape from their bad air, because they probably will not tack on you. On the other hand, if you are headed and the other boats are tacking away, hold your course for several extra boat lengths to clear your wind.

Keep in mind that after dipping a starboard-tack boat, you now have the advantage, because you will be on starboard the next time the two boats cross. Try to set up your starboard-tack advantages for approaching windward marks and the finish line.

There are several maneuvers that can prevent boats from tacking on your air. First, if you are going to windward and you want to keep another boat from tacking on your wind, slowly head your boat up just as the other boat is crossing your bow. (Diagram 61) It will appear not to have crossed your bow, and your competitor will likely wait to tack, clear of your wind. Trim your sails as you head up, keeping a slight leeward heel, so that it appears that you are sailing normally to windward. When the boat that is crossing you finally tacks, drive off for speed. You should be in clear air.

On the other hand, if you want a boat that is about to cross you to tack early, so that you are not blanketed, head off, say, three or four boat lengths before it crosses you, keeping the boat flat and your sails in. (Diagram 62) Do not act sneaky; just sail normally. As the boat crosses you, it will tack early. Once it begins the tack, head back up into the wind on your normal course and you will have clear air. This technique works particularly well near the lay lines.

If you are just making a mark and you want the boat ahead to undershoot that mark, head down, so that it will tack early. If you are already overstanding the mark and you want a boat to sail past you and overstand the mark by a greater distance, head up and the other boat will sail both beyond your wind and well beyond the mark. This will help cut the other boat's lead.

Valuable distance can easily be gained as you approach the windward mark. As the boats begin to funnel together there, many sailors make bad errors, leaving themselves with bad air and decreasing speeds. Since you have already planned your approach, you can concentrate on speed.

When approaching a windward mark to be rounded to port, a fleet is generally well organized, because all the boats are stacking up on starboard tack on the lay line and bearing off as they pass the mark. (Diagram 63) If you are on or above the lay line, you have the advantage of clear air for most of the way into the mark. When making the final tack for the windward mark, and provided you are within ten to fifteen boat lengths of the mark, as a general rule overshoot it by about one to one and a half boat lengths. Always try to approach the windward mark on the favored tack, so that on your final approach you will gain distance over boats sailing on a header. Try not to go to the lay line too early, because it is difficult to judge it from a distance. Also, any shift there can have a disastrous effect on you. If you get headed when very close to the mark, you may have to tack, and the boats behind will gain if they are again lifted up as they approach the mark. These extra tacks will cost you a lot of ground. (Diagram 64) In one race in 1977, *Enterprise* made up about ten boat lengths because *Courageous* was forced to make two extra tacks approaching a windward mark. We could

131

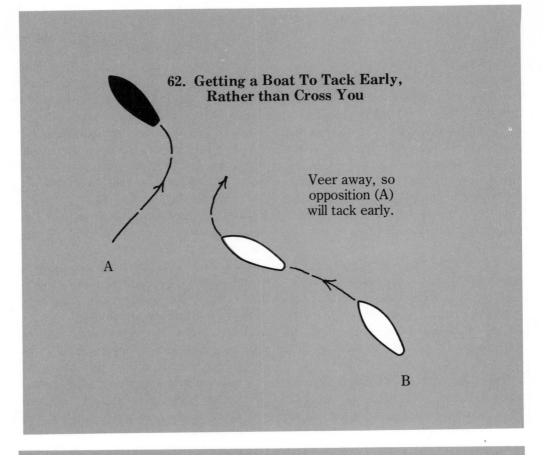

62. Getting a Boat To Tack Early, Rather than Cross You

Veer away, so opposition (A) will tack early.

A

B

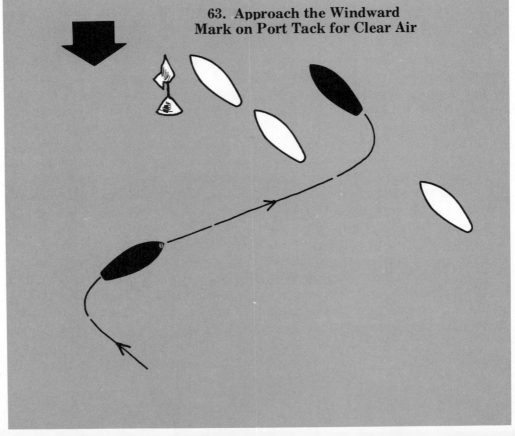

63. Approach the Windward Mark on Port Tack for Clear Air

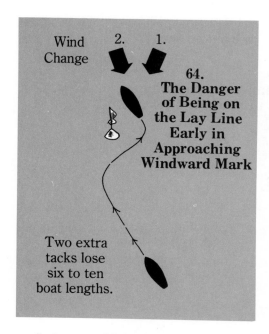

Wind Change

2.   1.

64. The Danger of Being on the Lay Line Early in Approaching Windward Mark

Two extra tacks lose six to ten boat lengths.

easily have avoided this problem by over-standing the mark by about one or two boat lengths. Overstanding a windward mark helps make for a better rounding, because your sheets are slightly eased off and you are moving fast as you bear off. If you over-stand, you may also sail around a stack of boats at the mark.

When you round the mark, look to see if there is extra anchor line let out that might be floating on the surface. If there is, it could easily be caught in your center-board, keel, or rudder and be dragged with your boat, forcing you to round the mark again.

If you have a lee bow current, you can sometimes "crab" the boat to windward by taking bites to fetch the mark. On the other hand, if the current is setting you to lee-ward and you are just barely making the mark, it is better to make two extra tacks early, to ensure you'll make the mark, rather than to try tacking just once, from a long distance, and wind up hitting the mark.

Practice shooting marks and objects in the water from different distances. Gener-ally in a centerboard boat, you can shoot the boat to windward effectively, without losing all your speed, for only about one boat length. In a keelboat such as a twelve-meter, you can shoot the boat to windward between two and four boat lengths and maintain your speed. In one race in 1977 between *Independence* and *Enterprise*, the two boats shot a mark from about three boat lengths to leeward, and ended up some two or three boat lengths to windward of the buoy. It is important when shooting that you do not allow your jib to back, slowing you down and forcing you to tack. Let the jib luff while you trim the mainsail. Keep the boat flat or just slightly heeled to lee-ward when shooting. If you heel to wind-ward, the boat will make leeway and could slide into the mark.

To take advantage of your right of way, it is always better to approach the windward mark on starboard tack if it is to be rounded to port. A mark that is to be rounded to starboard is also better approached on star-board because the starboard tacker gets to pick when to tack. Any boat on port tack must maneuver to get out of his way. (Dia-gram 65)

If you do find yourself on port tack ap-proaching a mark to be rounded to star-board, and encounter some boats on star-board tack, the best thing is to dip their sterns by heading at them, so that they can-not tack. Then round the mark. If the star-board-tack competitor has been smarter than that and set himself up so that if you dip him you end up to leeward of the mark, the next thing is to slow down by luffing and wait for the starboard tacker to go around. Then follow his stern around. (Diagram 66) The worst thing to do is to tack to starboard to stay clear of the starboard-tack boat.

Then you will be forced to tack again to port to round the mark, and you may find a second starboard tacker coming in that you will have to stay clear of.

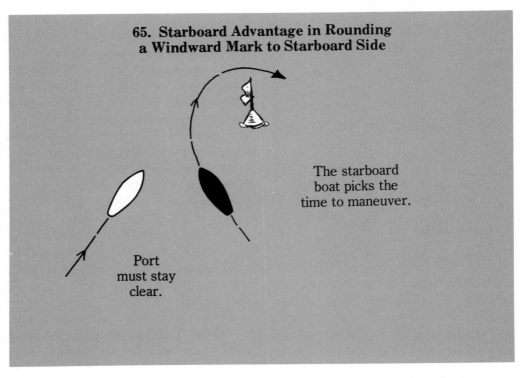

65. Starboard Advantage in Rounding a Windward Mark to Starboard Side

The starboard boat picks the time to maneuver.

Port must stay clear.

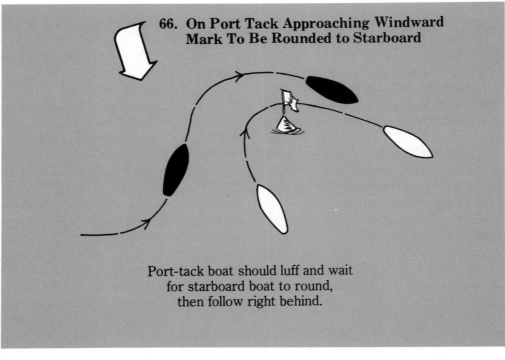

66. On Port Tack Approaching Windward Mark To Be Rounded to Starboard

Port-tack boat should luff and wait for starboard boat to round, then follow right behind.

Working Your Opponent Below the Lay Line
at a Windward Mark

If you have an opponent slightly to leeward and behind you as you approach the windward mark, you can drive him below the lay line by bearing off and sitting on his air. (Diagram 67) Keep heading down until you can barely make the mark. You will force the other boat to sail lower to clear his wind, and he will have to make extra tacks. This tactic is particularly effective in larger keelboats.

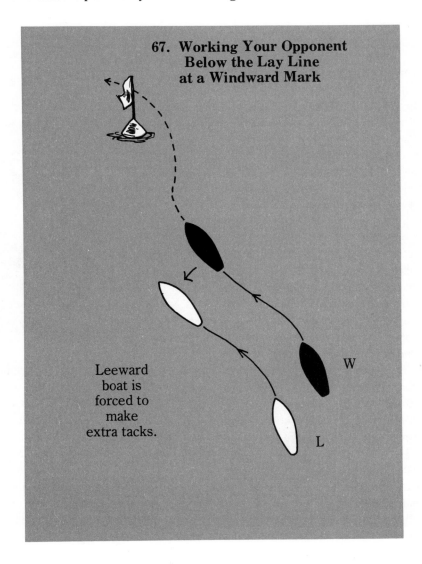

67. Working Your Opponent Below the Lay Line at a Windward Mark

Leeward boat is forced to make extra tacks.

W

L

Rounding the Windward Mark; Sailing the Leeward Leg

ually around the mark. We have already discussed overstanding by one to one and a half boat lengths; this tactic keeps the course change to a minimum, allowing you to bear off slightly early, about one to two boat lengths from the windward mark.

If the leeward leg is straight downwind, you should note whether you need to bear away or to jibe around the windward mark. Generally, it is better to bear away, because you do lose speed in a jibe. If you are trying to decide between a jibe spinnaker set and a bear-away set, bear away, as a rule, unless the leeward leg is favored on the opposite jibe by about twenty degrees. If you are not sure, always bear away, because you will have the option of jibing once the boat is up to full speed. It may be a good idea to jibe over, however, so that you gain the inside advantage at the next mark, where you will also be the leeward boat. Jibing may clear your boat from the blanketing zones of boats rounding behind you. If you find that you are making a tack set around the windward mark, do not start pulling the spinnaker up until after the tack is completed and the sails are eased out. This will keep the spinnaker from going into the water when the genoa jib is trimmed tight.

Any mark rounding is easiest and fastest with as small a course change as possible. The greater the change in course, the more your boat will slow down. One way to avoid making major course changes when rounding the windward mark is to bear off grad-

Once you have made your approach to the windward mark, start the rounding by keeping the boat flat, or "under the mast." This allows you to keep the boat under control while you maneuver, bearing off quickly to increase speed without losing distance. To keep the boat "under the mast," ease the main and jib out rapidly while rounding. An overtrimmed mainsail will prevent the boat from bearing off, and if you let the boat heel, the centerboard will begin to cavitate (air will be trapped between the hull and the

His boat heeling too much as it rounds the windward mark, this Contender sailor is having difficulty bearing off. Dumping the main out farther with a loose boomvang would help.

Rule 42.3A: "A yacht clear astern may establish an inside overlap and be entitled to room under Rule 42.1A . . . only when the yacht clear ahead: (i) is able and (ii) is outside two of her overall lengths of the mark *except when either yacht has completed a tack within two overall lengths of the mark.*" In other words, if there is a boat that has tacked in the vicinity of the mark, the two-boat-lengths determinative rule will not apply. (Diagrams 68 and 69)

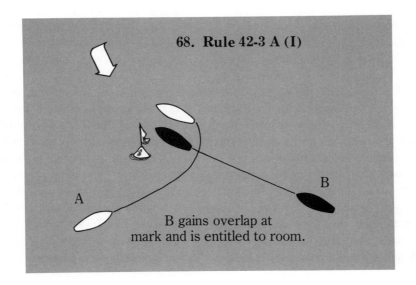

68. Rule 42-3 A (I)

B gains overlap at
mark and is entitled to room.

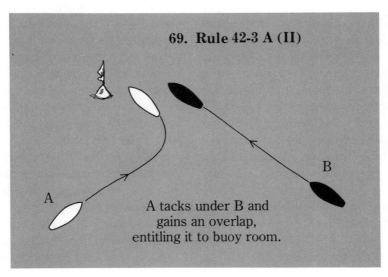

69. Rule 42-3 A (II)

A tacks under B and
gains an overlap,
entitling it to buoy room.

centerboard, making the rudder ineffective and throwing the boat off balance).

In a two-man boat, one member of the crew must keep hiking and watching the boat, while the other concentrates on getting the spinnaker up; if both crew members have their heads wrapped up in halyards and adjustments, they are asking for trouble. During the actual rounding, it is better to concentrate on speed than to worry about getting the spinnaker up, pulling the board up, or making minor adjustments.

Many sailors try to fly the spinnaker too early. Don't be in a hurry. It's more important to concentrate on speed, keeping the wind slightly forward of the beam. A neat trick in light air is to keep the apparent wind at about eighty-five degrees, with your spinnaker pole just off the headstay. This tactic increases the maximum apparent wind in the sail. It works well in all boats, especially planing boats. Flying Dutchman sailors, even on straight downwind legs, will keep the pole well forward, sailing on reaches back and forth. They gain more than enough speed to compensate for the extra distance.

In one race between *Courageous* and *Enterprise*, with *Courageous* ahead, we set our spinnaker only to find that we lost so much speed while doing so that *Enterprise*, by keeping her genoa jib working, sailed over the top of us and went on to take the lead. Often in a planing dinghy, sailors will sail a high course to keep their wind clear after a windward mark. At this time it is better to concentrate on planing and going fast before you start to get your spinnaker up.

Remember: boat speed first; sail trim second; other adjustments third.

After rounding the windward mark, many sailors get thrown off by following the leader, who is often twenty to forty degrees off course. The crew should immediately inquire of the skipper, "Do you see the next mark?" and if he does not, somebody should be assigned to spot it.

Once around the mark, make a fast getaway. Haul up the spinnaker, adjust your sails, and settle in for pure speed. Often, sailors work hard on the windward legs only to relax downwind. But this is the opportunity to get really tough and to make up as much ground as possible on the leaders or, if you are in the lead, to get away from the fleet. Your getaway at this point sets the stage for your approach to the next mark.

If you are on a reach and planning to go over a boat ahead of you, you have to do this at a key time. On a leeward leg, it is better to pass early to windward and then, later in the leg, to pass to leeward. It is important to stay about one to two boat lengths away from a leeward boat, because the boat to leeward always has the right to luff (Rule 37). To sail over a leeward boat make your move subtly, so that the other boat cannot make a large alteration and luff you drastically off course. Sail over the boat ahead of you when you have a lot of speed—say, in the beginning of a puff or when the other boat is not yet moving fast. If the other boat is moving slowly, you will be able to sail right by when it finally tries to luff you.

The *helmsman* must call "mast abeam" as soon as you are in this position. (Diagram 70) This compels the leeward boat to sail on its proper course—the fastest course to the next mark, which is normally the course the leeward boat would be sailing in the absence of the windward boat.

On a reach or a run, there are several effective ways to pass to leeward of a boat. First, if you are running, try to sail as far

With both boats on parallel courses, skipper of 97 is in mast-abeam position.

70. The Mast Abeam Position

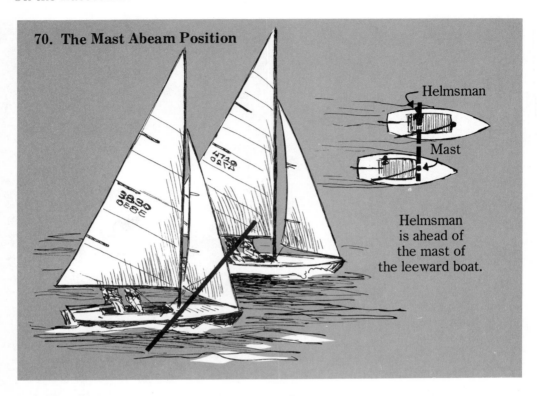

Helmsman

Mast

Helmsman is ahead of the mast of the leeward boat.

71. Rule 39

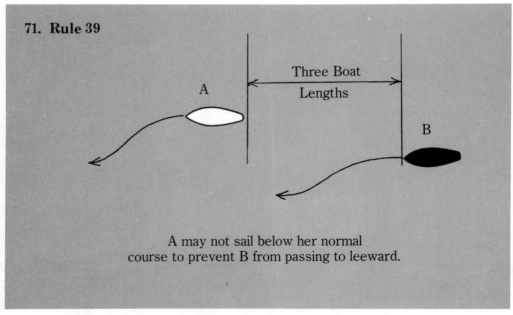

A

Three Boat Lengths

B

A may not sail below her normal course to prevent B from passing to leeward.

to leeward of the windward boat as you can. Under the rules (Rule 39: Same Tack—Sailing Below a Proper Course), "a yacht which is on a free leg of a course shall not sail below her proper course when she is clearly within three of her overall lengths of either a leeward yacht or a yacht clear astern which is steering a course to pass to leeward." (Diagram 71)

You can gain speed by taking dives to leeward when you get puffs. Watch the telltales of the windward boat to judge whether or not your wind is clear. Again, keep in mind that the wind shadow of a windward boat extends between four and six mast lengths, depending on the wind conditions. When you have sailed well to leeward of the windward boat and you are about abeam of it, it is time to sail through. To do this, you need to increase speed and to spend as little time as possible in the wind shadow of the windward boat. Just as his masthead fly is

pointing at you, harden up to a reach, making a slow alteration of course to increase your speed, and sail across the wind shadow. (Diagram 72) Once you are through his wind shadow (you can determine this by your relative speed and by watching the other boat's telltales), bear off and resume your course down the leg.

You can make up valuable ground on a boat ahead of you by continually changing course, though keep in mind that this may cause you to lose ground to the leaders. Sail directly astern of the boat ahead, and slowly begin reaching up to force the boat ahead to react to you by luffing. As soon as he is on your course or slightly higher, slowly bear off again to your normal course. Come up when you have a light-wind spot, and go off as you get a puff. The boat ahead will react to you instead of to the wind, and you will be able to reduce the lead by about half a boat length on every alteration of

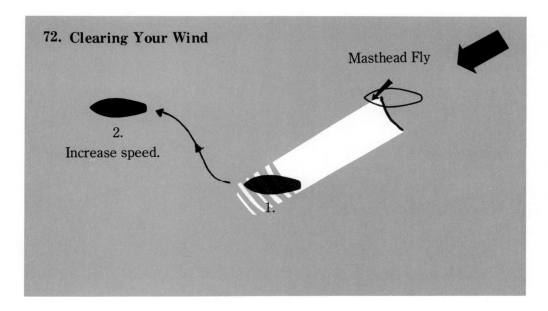

72. Clearing Your Wind

Masthead Fly

2.
Increase speed.

1.

Sailing by Air Speed vs. Boat Speed

In big-boat racing you may find it advantageous, as we did on *Courageous*, to sail downwind according to air speed instead of boat speed. The reason: the instrumentation is more sensitive to air speed than to boat speed.

If you are sailing a leeward leg and your boat speed increases, you will be able to bear off and sail a little lower course while maintaining your original speed. The problem, however, is that you could have done this before your knot meter indicated an increase in boat speed. You are always reacting to the puff about thirty to forty-five seconds late, after its effects register on the instrument.

Sailing by air speed is better. For example, if the air speed over the anemometer is 10.29 knots on a particular course and the wind goes up to 10.7 knots, you know that you have a puff and that your boat speed is going to increase. So as the puff hits, you can immediately start to bear off, and you will maintain your boat speed. The trick here is to establish an average air speed or apparent wind over the deck from astern, and then maintain your speed by scalloping to leeward ("taking dives"). Sailing by air speed, you will be able to gain at least three to five boat lengths on a three-or-four-mile downwind leg.

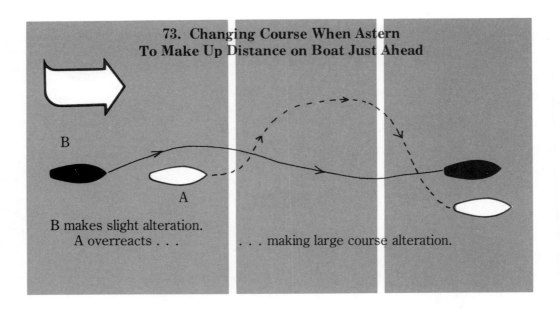

**73. Changing Course When Astern
To Make Up Distance on Boat Just Ahead**

B

A

B makes slight alteration.
A overreacts . . .

. . . making large course alteration.

course. (Diagram 73) You can effectively work a boat off to one side of a course by this method. Always jibe first, so that you cross the wind of the boat ahead on your way to the mark while the other boat is caught sailing in your bad air.

It helps when sailing downwind if you can keep a boat trapped in your blanketing zone. You do so by sailing at the same speed as the leeward boat. You can trap a boat and keep it sailing away from the mark until you pick when you want to jibe. You can also catch a boat ahead by sailing on its wind from behind. This technique will work well with any boat.

As a general rule on leeward legs, jibe on the lifts. You are lifted downwind when the apparent wind comes aft while you maintain the same course. For example, you have been lifted if you find that you need to trim your pole aft and ease your sails more to sail the same course. It is at this point that you want to jibe. When you

jibe, keep your speed at a maximum. Always jibe so that you are sailing the favored course downwind. (Diagram 74) Use your compass to differentiate between the course you are sailing and the course to the mark versus the course you would have to sail on the other jibe to make the mark. By simply observing where the leeward mark is, you can judge which jibe is closer. The course that seems to take you there the fastest is the one that you want to sail. Stand up and look around occasionally for the breeze that is coming, so that you can anticipate what is going to happen.

Rounding the Reach Mark and the Leeward Mark

As you approach a reach mark, it is important to establish buoy room. Make a mental note of what the apparent wind is going to be on the second reach leg. If you find that the leg is going to be pretty much dead downwind, it may be better to stay on the outside of the fleet at the reach mark, so that you will have a better angle on the leg and not be caught in any early luffing matches. However, if you find that the second reach leg is going to be close to the wind, it is critical to establish buoy room, so that you are not caught to leeward and behind boats reaching over the top of you.

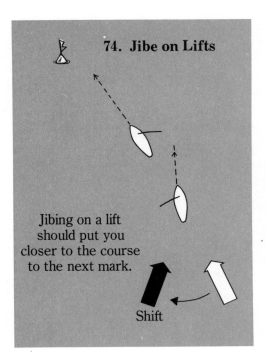

74. Jibe on Lifts

Jibing on a lift should put you closer to the course to the next mark.

Shift

75. Protecting Your Position Downwind

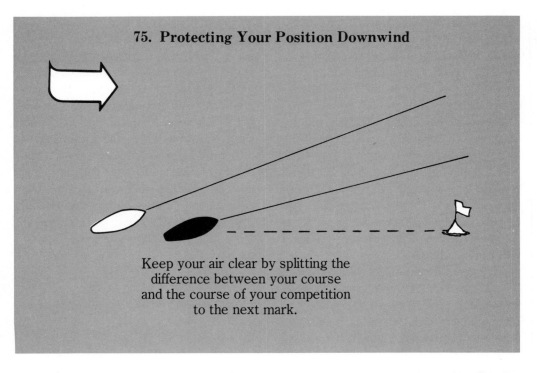

Keep your air clear by splitting the
difference between your course
and the course of your competition
to the next mark.

76. Jibing To Break an Overlap

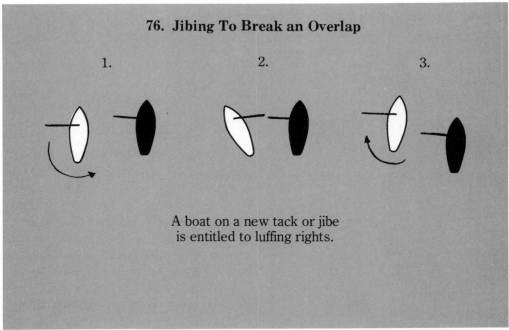

A boat on a new tack or jibe
is entitled to luffing rights.

There are several ways to break an overlap when sailing downwind. First, you can sail clear ahead of a windward boat. But this is often difficult, because you may fall into the blanketing zone of that boat. A second way is to reestablish luffing rights whenever you are on a new tack or jibe. One can effect this downwind by jibing away and then jibing back. (Diagram 76) A third technique is to sail two overall lengths of the longer yacht away from the windward boat.

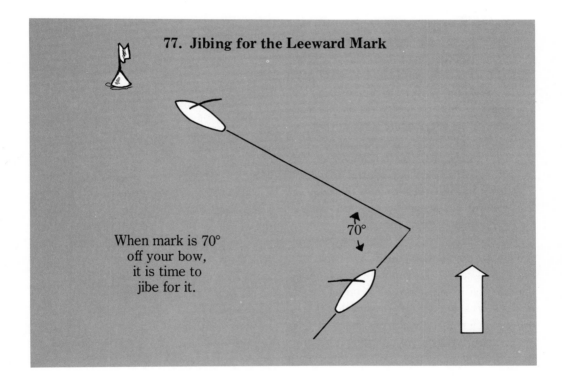

77. Jibing for the Leeward Mark

When mark is 70° off your bow, it is time to jibe for it.

70°

In the Laser class, this lineup is called "the passing lane." You should try to stay in the passing lane.

The most important thing to consider approaching a leeward mark is where you are going to be after the mark rounding. Note what your rhumb lines are. Using your compass, note the number of degrees you are jibing through. For example, if you are jibing through seventy degrees, you know that you are on the rhumb line when the mark bears seventy degrees away from your course. (Diagram 77) It is important not to jibe early for the leeward mark, because you will be caught sailing downwind and making a slow approach and a slower rounding.

When sailing downwind, you should keep in

mind five critically important concepts:
1) Always keep your air clear.
2) Sail the favored course to the next mark.
3) Never let your boat go slower than the boats around you.
4) Use your starboard and leeward advantages to prevent boats from staying on your wind.
5) When a boat is trying to pass to windward of you, protect your position by splitting the difference between your course to the next mark and the course that the other boat is sailing. (Diagram 75) To keep your air clear when you are in this position, you must know where the boat to windward and behind is getting its wind. Never sail a course higher than the boat to windward and behind unless you are making a sharp luff. If you do head higher, you are losing distance to the next mark. Conversely, if you are the boat behind and to windward, you will want to trap the boat to leeward and ahead by having it sail a course higher than yours.

The first rule when making your approach to the leeward mark is always to have good speed. To generate speed coming into the mark, approach it on as much of a reach as you can. If you find that there are a number of boats already ahead of you at the mark, slow down, either by luffing or by altering your course, so that you don't get caught in the pack. Try to end up on the inside quarter of the boat that is ahead of you. In this manner, you will have trapped the boats to leeward and ahead, because they cannot tack. You will also have clear air or, at worst, be sailing in some backwind, but at least you will not be blanketed. Never allow yourself to be caught to leeward and behind at a leeward mark.

When making the rounding, keep the centerboard up slightly, so that the boat

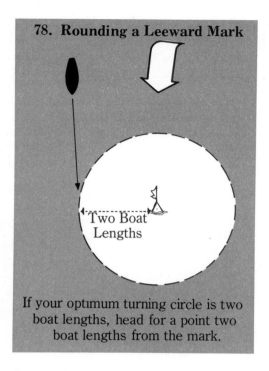

78. Rounding a Leeward Mark

Two Boat Lengths

If your optimum turning circle is two boat lengths, head for a point two boat lengths from the mark.

does not stall. Trim your sails as you round up, moving the tiller as little as you can. Finally and most important, keep the boat flat or sailing on its lines. Under the rules, you may make a seamanlike rounding, which we consider to be about one to one and a half boat lengths from the mark. This allows you a tactical rounding—you go wide on one side of the mark and come up close to the second side. Try to have your boat set up for sailing to windward before you get to the leeward mark, so that you can concentrate on sailing and speed once you have rounded it. Do not worry about little things like storing the spinnaker pole, adjusting the cunningham, or minor sail trim. Worry about minor adjustments later.

Again, keep in mind that the greater the course change, the more you will slow down. Try to approach the mark on a reach, making your optimum turning circle (Diagram 78), which is as small as possible, without losing speed to get around the

In rounding leeward mark, Jobson trims the mainsheet by passing it from one hand to the other without letting go of tiller.

mark. If you are reaching and you put the jib up, you will not lose much speed if the spinnaker comes down early. If, however, you are sailing downwind, straight to the mark, you may find it advantageous to free-float the spinnaker for several boat lengths before making a rounding. The sail will stay full while your crew gets the pole stowed.

Trim the spinnaker well out to windward, so that it won't collapse while you are putting up your jib.

After Rounding the Leeward Mark

Once you have rounded the leeward mark, the next thing to consider is the first tack

to make a fast getaway. Many people feel that tacking away from the leeward mark immediately is a good thing, but be careful that you are not sailing underneath the spinnakers of boats coming downwind. It may be better to sail for several boat lengths first, gaining your speed before you tack away to clear your wind. If it looks as if boats ahead of you are going to tack early, it may be better to tack right away or to let them tack and to sail on into clear air. On the other hand, if you think that the left side of the course is favored, then go left early. Just as you need to avoid making too many tacks after the start, it is also important not to make too many tacks after rounding the leeward mark. Sailing in bad air for a short time can lose you far less distance to the leaders than can several extra tacks.

Make your first tack count. Decide before coming to the leeward mark which side of the course is favored, so that you can plan the next windward leg. You will already have learned this by sailing one windward leg and watching the boats around you. Make a note early on the beat whether you

are gaining on that side of the course or losing distance to the boats on the other side. This will give you an early indication of which side of the course is going to be favored. As a rule, if the boats are getting more wind to the left of you than to the right of you, it may be a good time to tack over to the left to cover the fleet.

Do not allow yourself to be trapped on the wings of the course. Use other boats on your racecourse to determine what the wind is doing. On *Courageous*, if we saw a day sailer ahead pointing ten degrees higher, it was an indication that we were going to get a lift.

Try not to be involved with individual boats on this leg, since you are really trying to concentrate on moving up on the leaders. Do not tack until you are sure you should.

The Finish

In making the final sprint to the finish line, your approach can make the difference between victory and defeat in close competition. There are several rules to follow when finishing:

1) If you are finishing up at the starting line and one end was favored there, the other end will be favored at the finish. (Diagram 79) If you are finishing at a new line, you can determine which end of the line is favored by noting the angle of the flags on the committee boat or on the course itself. Keep in mind that bright orange buoys sometimes appear closer than they are.

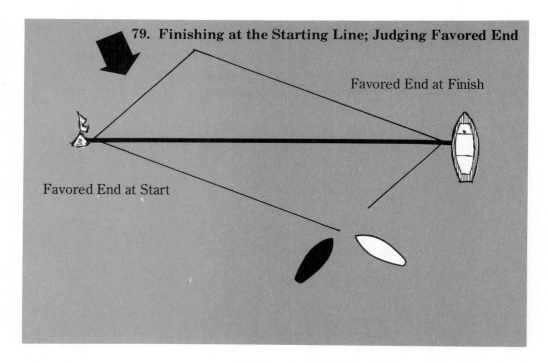

79. Finishing at the Starting Line; Judging Favored End

Favored End at Finish

Favored End at Start

Solings cross finish line on favored, port tack. In finishing one should plan to be on favored tack and at the favored end.

2) Avoid, if possible, finishing in the middle of the line; the race-committee member sighting the line generally looks at the far end as his reference point, particularly when the committee boat has a high vantage point, so he may miss boats in the middle of the line.

3) Always cross the finish line on the favored tack. If you are undecided whether port or starboard tack is favored, choose starboard, because you have the advantage coming into it of forcing other boats to maneuver around you.

4) Avoid tacking at the finish line if you can, unless you are right at the finish mark.

Shooting the line works best if you are the windward boat gaining bearing on the boat to leeward. *Courageous* won a race against *Enterprise* by half a second only because we shot the line just a split second better than *Enterprise*, which shot a little bit too early and consequently was losing speed as it crossed.

The Enterprise crew closed their bearing with the windward boat and lost distance to the line. Do not shoot the line if you are leeward unless your stern is about even with the bow of the windward boat.

Make your approach so that you will be sailing in clear air for a long time and not making any tacks at the finish line.

Under the rules, you finish when any part of your hull, crew, or sails crosses the line. Keep in mind that you must clear the finish line before putting on your engine.

Part 4

Match Racing

special strategies for special races

Match racing is different from most kinds of sailing, because your tactics are governed more by the other boat than by the wind. Boat handling and maneuvering become more important, and generally the crew that handles its boat better will win. With such a premium on the work of the crew, the bigger the boat the more difficult the match race. This is part of the challenge and thrill of twelve-meter match racing.

Since there is more maneuvering than in fleet racing, match racing is good practice for any fleet racer, offering the chance to master skills such as tacking, jibing, mark rounding, and playing wind shifts. Match racing also provides an opportunity to judge boat speed one-on-one.

The main match races in this country are the America's Cup, the Congressional Cup, and the Prince of Wales Bowl. There are also several regional match-race-type regattas, including the Taylor Trophy on Long Island Sound, the Richardson Cup on the Great Lakes, and the Douglas Cup in collegiate sailing.

Most match races are set up with the boats assigned to opposite ends of the starting line. They race to a windward mark, down to a leeward mark, and back up to the finish. Windward-leeward match-race courses are best, because straight downwind runs offer more tactical possibilities than do reaching legs.

First of all, to avoid errors, understand what the course is. In the Congressional Cup, for example, there is a rule that you must sail through the starting line on your second windward leg. We nearly forgot this in 1978, and almost cost ourselves the race. Only a crew member's offhand comment about it saved the day.

The most important thing in match racing is to establish a lead, because the most difficult thing is to regain the lead once it has been lost. For this reason, be sure to tune your boat well before the start, sailing a good distance up the windward break to get in tune with the waves and changing patterns of the wind. On *Courageous* we generally spend about an hour getting ready before each start, taking wind readings (direction and velocity), tuning our boat, putting the leads into position, and getting used to steering and sailing to windward. To start racing on a course where you have not first tuned up is to just about cripple your chances for gaining that all-important early lead.

It is also important to know the weather, so that you do not miss any shifts and you have the right sails up at the right time.

Mastering the Start

Traditionally, boats begin circling with each other at some point to leeward of the line, each trying to control the other. One controls one's competitor by staying between him and the line.

Make your circles in a clockwise direction. If you are the boat approaching on starboard, try to pass to leeward of the boat on port. This makes it easier to gain the stern of the port tacker, and the port-tack boat will not be able to throw a reversal (see next page) easily. As you are about to make circles with the competition, approach with as much speed as you can. The fastest course in sailing is the beam reach; therefore, in the last two to three boat lengths before engaging the other boat, try to get your boat on as much of a beam reach as

Opening spread: Courageous *rounds leeward mark in second race* against Australia *eleven seconds ahead, smallest margin of the series.*

you can. Sail on a broad reach if you are going to jibe, on a close reach if you are about to pass. Try to make your circles as large as you can, keeping up your speed. The circles will become ellipses, allowing the sails to be filled for a longer time and the boat to regain speed before you make your next maneuver. When you make your circles, try to stay within the lay lines of the starting mark.

Know how long it takes to sail your starting line from one end to the other. In case you get on a chase along the line or if you are going for the start, you will know how much time you have before the gun goes off. Also know what your lay lines are, so that you will not be trapped outside them during the start. (Diagram 80)

If the windward, or starboard, end of the line is favored, attempt to be the windward boat, working your opponent down to the port end. If the port end of the starting line is favored, you should be the leeward boat approaching the line, trying to work your

opponent toward the starboard end.

If the boats are assigned to opposite ends of the line, try to meet your competitor directly downwind of the line, approaching him from leeward.

If your opposition will not engage you, sail up to him, tack in front of him, lead him to the committee boat, and begin making circles around the committee boat. (The bigger the committee boat, the more potent a weapon it is.) At some point—say, after two complete circles—reverse your direction, so that you approach the boat on starboard tack. Try to make a better rounding underneath the committee boat than your competitor does, so that you get on his inside windward quarter, preventing him from making a tack to go around once again.

Instead of starting out by circling as you make your approach to another boat coming from the opposite end of the line, you might consider throwing a "reversal." If your opponent tacks around, head back up instead of jibing and becoming the leeward boat.

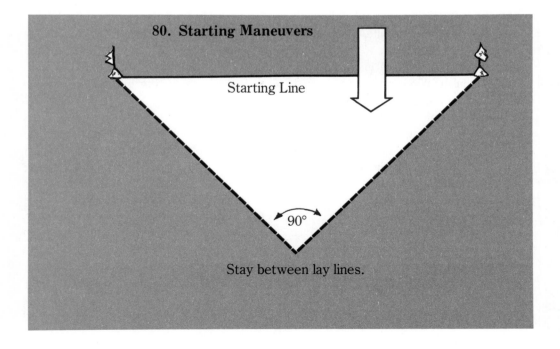

80. Starting Maneuvers

Starting Line

90°

Stay between lay lines.

This technique is effective on all boats. The defense is to throw a reversal yourself, so that both boats reverse their patterns and a circle then starts the other way. Or both boats will be tacking away from each other. In this case try to be the boat to leeward, so that on your next approach you will again be the boat coming from leeward position. This way you have more maneuverability and the leeward right-of-way as well.

As a cardinal rule, never stop moving before the start. If you do you may become stuck in irons and your competitor will control you. Also, never allow yourself to go to windward of the line unless your opponent is to windward of you. If you find that you are in trouble, start maneuvering immediately to clear it up. You can escape a competitor by using spectator boats or marker buoys. Get him as close to your stern as you can. When he commits himself to one side or the other of a mark, simply go the other way and you have escaped. (Diagram 81)

Another method of escaping from an opponent is crabbing to windward. Luff your boat almost head to wind without stopping and try to capture the air of the boat behind you. As the boat behind falls into your wind shadow, take another bite to windward and get on his wind. You are now to windward and ahead, and you can tack freely, staying on his wind to keep him late for the line. If you are the boat behind in this situation, speed up, so that you can sail through the wind shadow and be bow to bow with the boat to windward of you, luffing it, holding it up, and then being the first to go for speed at the start. In a match race, always be the first boat going for speed—having clear air and accelerating for the line. Never be early, trying to slow down for the line, because the other boat will break through. If you find that you are going to be over the line early or that you are going to be pushed from one end of the line to the other, bail out early to minimize your loss.

Luffing is a relatively new technique at

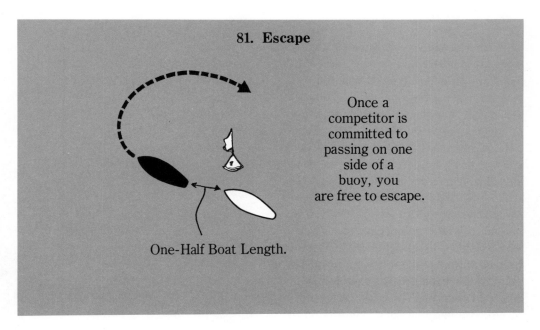

81. Escape

Once a competitor is committed to passing on one side of a buoy, you are free to escape.

One-Half Boat Length.

the start of match races, used successfully in 1977 by all the twelve-meters. The theory is that you can control a boat as well from ahead as from behind. Luff up sharply, so that your competitor rounds up and gets overlapped on your inside, leaving you room to bear off and jibe away for a clear approach back to the line. This principle works well as long as both boats keep moving—and in fact, the twelve-meters never went slower than about four and a half knots, even though their jibs were luffing most of the time.

Windward Tactics

Once the starting gun has gone off, the two boats are probably on the same tack. If the boats are on opposite tacks and you think you are heading the right way or that you are ahead, you should probably tack over to cover at some point—say, after five to ten boat lengths. If you are behind or think you are going the wrong way, you should immediately tack and initiate a tacking duel. If the two boats are about even, one will eventually establish a lead, forcing the other boat to tack away and begin a tacking duel. Always initiate a tacking duel when you are dead downwind of the windward mark (Diagram 82), to keep yourself centered on the course. Otherwise you could be forced to make extra tacks or sail a long way on the lay line.

Courageous *and* Australia *(KA5) duel to windward. In this
situation* Courageous *might have forced* Australia *to tack
had she tacked earlier herself, blocking* Australia's *wind.*

157

Opposite *and* above: Courageous *takes a five-degree
bite to windward to backwind* Australia's *sails*.

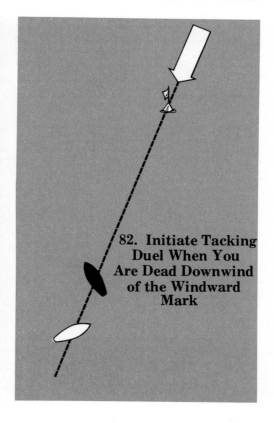

82. Initiate Tacking Duel When You Are Dead Downwind of the Windward Mark

In a tacking duel, the boat ahead tries to stay in phase with the boat behind, always on its wind, never allowing it to keep clear. The boat ahead should begin to tack on the wind of the boat behind when the latter is beyond head-to-wind. By bearing off slightly, the boat ahead can actually be close-reaching going from tack to tack, keeping up its speed to slow down its competitor. (Diagram 83) The boat ahead simply waits until it is up to full speed, then tacks to cover, and the boat behind will have the unhappy choice of either tacking to get out of phase, losing further distance, or holding on and losing about four lengths.

The goal of the boat ahead is to increase its lead by making better tacks, favoring the better side of the course and forcing the boat behind to the other. If, for example,

159

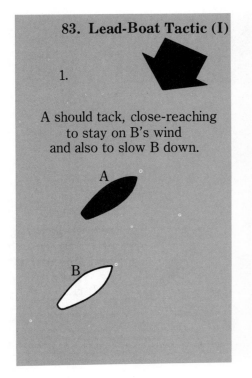

83. Lead-Boat Tactic (I)

1.

A should tack, close-reaching
to stay on B's wind
and also to slow B down.

A

B

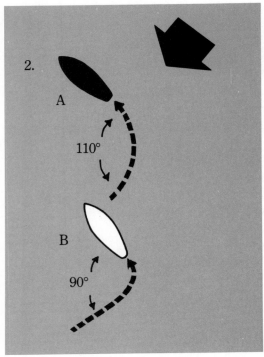

2.

A

110°

B

90°

the wind is better to the right, then the boat ahead tries to push the boat behind to the left. Thus, when the boat behind is to the left and on port tack heading for the right side of the course, the boat ahead, on starboard tack and heading to the left, tacks directly on its air, forcing it to tack away to the left. (Diagram 84) Once up to speed, the boat ahead tacks to cover, herding the boat behind to the left by giving it clear air as it is going that way. Eventually, the boat behind will tack to port to try to get back in the course, whereupon the boat ahead tacks on its air again, forcing it to tack away again to the unfavored left side.

The boat ahead should try not to overreact to the boat behind, keeping in mind what the wind as well as what the other boat is doing. If, for example, you are sailing on a seven-degree lift and your competitor has just tacked away, it may be better to hold on for several boat lengths,

waiting to get headed slightly before tacking to cover.

The basic principle in tacking duels, for boats both ahead and behind, is simple: *Never tack unless you are going as fast as or faster than the other boat.*

For the boat behind, the tactics are more challenging, because it has not only to initiate tacking duels but to sail in bad air from time to time to do so. The first thing to do is get out of phase with the tacking routine of the boat ahead of you. You can achieve this by making double or triple tacks, so that the boat ahead cannot keep up with you. Start your first tack when you are up to full speed by close-reaching. After completing it, and when the windward boat has gone beyond head-to-wind in tacking in response, start tacking again. Once the windward boat has started tacking back and has gone past head-to-wind making this second tack, make a third tack. At this point you will be out of phase, though it will have cost you two to four boat lengths to get there.

At this point your objective is to regain the lead, and you can do it by making better tacks, approaching your competitor with speed as your boats converge, and tacking away late when he tacks on you. The routine goes something like this:

A boat is crossing you and is about to tack on your wind. Wait until it has just about completed its tack and you are going at about the same speed. At this point, tack away. When up to speed, the other boat will follow, tacking to cover you. You immediately tack away again. In this manner, you give yourself the opportunity to make better tacks than the competition, since you are initiating them while sailing at the same speed. Your goal is to progress sufficiently so that when you are on port tack the starboard-tack boat can no longer tack on you without coming too close. It is at this point that you dip the stern of the starboard-tack

boat and start heading for the other side of the course, so that you will have the starboard advantage the next time the two boats approach each other. The boat ahead will tack under your leeward bow as a defense, but this simply means that you are on the verge of overtaking him. The next time the boats converge you may be ahead and even be tacking on the other boat.

Unless you happen to catch your competitor sleeping, a false tack usually works against rather than for you as a tactic for picking up distance once you are out of phase. The windward boat ahead will likely not tack on you unless you are beyond head-to-wind in your tack. So if you throw a false tack, going beyond head-to-wind and falling back off, the other boat simply tacks, follows through, and leaves you farther behind. The only thing the false tack accomplishes is to get you out of phase or, if you are ahead and out of phase, to get you back in phase.

84. Lead-Boat Tactic (II)

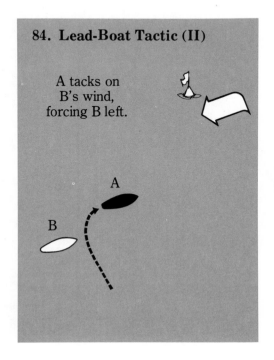

A tacks on B's wind, forcing B left.

Rounding the Windward Mark; the Downwind Leg

Once near the lay line, the boat ahead holds, heading for the windward mark and forcing the boat behind either to make extra tacks, which mean extra lost distance, or to sail in bad air all the way to the mark. It is best of all for the boat ahead when it can work the boat behind to the lower lay line, so that the boat ahead just barely makes a good, clean rounding and the boat behind is forced into extra tacks in order to negotiate the mark.

To defend against this, the boat behind must keep in mind its approach to the windward mark as it is working upwind. If you find that you are being worked to one side of the course or the other, you may want to hold for a time to work yourself back into the course. Holding is a good way of centering both boats.

Make your last tack on the lay line, or slightly overshoot as close to the mark as you can. By covering very closely at the rounding, the boat behind can sometimes force the boat ahead to make an extra tack, to make sure it will have clear air after the rounding.

When you are making your final approach to the windward mark, note which tack is favored. If the starboard tack is favored coming into the windward mark, this means the port jibe will be favored going to the leeward mark. In that case you may consider making a jibe set.

Once you have determined which jibe is favored, make your jibe set only if that tack is favored by at least fifteen to twenty degrees. To make a jibe set generally costs about two boat lengths, because you must bear away and jibe before setting the spinnaker, losing distance to a boat that goes with a bear-away set. In courses favoring the downwind leg twenty degrees or more, this two-boat-length loss is more than offset by the advantage of being on the favored course early.

If you are the lead boat going downwind,

keep your wind clear by splitting the difference between the course of the boat behind and your course to the next mark. (Note Diagram 75, page 144) Observe the masthead fly of the boat behind you to see where the wind is flowing. If you are the boat behind, you have the advantage at this point, because you are between the wind and the boat ahead. You can slow it down by getting on its wind, or forcing it to jibe and to cross your wind. Jibe so that your wind shadow is just ahead of the boat ahead. It will have to sail through it, after which it will either jibe away or continue heading higher than you, and in either case it is a net gain for you. (Diagram 85)

Once the boat ahead has gone through your wind, you as the trailing boat can bear off and sail your normal course again. Keep in mind downwind that you should jibe on the lift to stay on the favored jibe and in phase with the wind shifts, whereas the boat ahead must react to you.

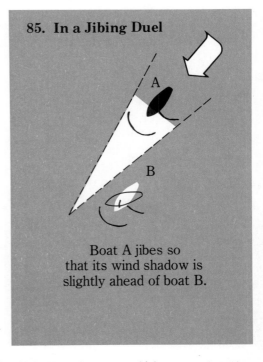

85. In a Jibing Duel

Boat A jibes so
that its wind shadow is
slightly ahead of boat B.

Cal 40 7077 reaches up to a higher course to capture the wind of 7124, forcing her to sail a longer leg.

Courageous *(26) bears away after luffing*
Independence, *causing her spinnaker to collapse.*

Rounding the Leeward Mark; the Finish

Try to work your position sailing downwind so that you will be approaching the leeward mark on the inside, entitling you to buoy room in the event of an overlap. If you realize that you are not going to have buoy room at the mark, head for a point on your turning circle—for example, two boat lengths from the mark if your optimum turning circle is two boat lengths. (Diagram 78, page 146) In this way you can make your rounding close aboard the mark while sailing to windward, losing as little speed as possible and leaving yourself free to tack immediately after the mark, trapping the boat ahead if it has not made a good rounding as well.

If you are the boat ahead coming around the leeward mark, you might take a sharp luff to windward so that you are to windward of the boat behind you. Then bear off for speed and be up to full speed as the boat behind comes around the mark. The boat ahead tacks simultaneously with the boat behind, trying to stay in phase with it and slow it down. You can slow down a boat behind you by constantly sailing across its wind, reaching back and forth. When you are still moving well and the boat behind is moving slowly, it is likely to make one more tack. At this point hold on and continue sailing until you are up to full speed; then tack to cover. This will force the boat behind

either to tack right away or once again to stay in phase. Generally this technique gains about four boat lengths in a match race.

Plan your approach to the finish line early, so that you will have a plan to follow as you make your final approach. If the race is close, put yourself in a position approaching the line so that you are the boat on the favored tack. Try not to maneuver near the finish line except for heading up if you are the inside boat. If you have a choice, finish at one end of the line or the other—not in the middle—and be on starboard so that the other boat has to maneuver around you. It is important to keep your cool coming into the finish line—don't clutch up.

Protests and Appeals

by Gary Jobson

If you are in the right, there is no reason to lose a protest. This is the concept of the International Yacht Racing Rules and the jury-hearing system—that justice should prevail. However, justice is generally not automatic; in most instances, you must work for it. When you are involved in a protest situation and are in the wrong, then it is your responsibility to drop out, or do a 720 if the racing instructions permit. But if you believe you are right, then it is up to you to take the steps necessary to ensure that justice is served.

Before getting into how to win your protest, there are two pieces of advice that are as old as they are true. First, *know your rules—frontwards, backwards, inside and out.* There is no substitute for knowing exactly where you stand in any racing situation. Ignorance of your rights and responsibilities or even a moment's indecision can lead to a great deal of trouble.

Second, *whenever possible, avoid getting involved in protests.* In spite of my opening statement, no matter how right you think you might be, there is always a chance that you might be disqualified. In judgment situations, slightly different views of the same incident can make it difficult to tell who was really right or wrong.

This is especially true in onus situations. For instance, you may be positive that you completed your tack before the other boat had to alter course, or that you established your overlap exactly two boat lengths from the jibe mark. But the rules say that the onus is on you to prove it, which can sometimes be tricky when it is a matter of a few feet or even inches. And don't forget that although most of the rules don't state the onus, some, such as the opposite tack rule, either imply or state in an appeal that the helmsman who is cutting it close has to prove that he made it. Although it some-

times pays to take a risk, you should fully realize that the consequences might include disqualification even if you are successful. Most of the time you are better off avoiding questionable situations and deciding the outcome of the race on the remaining legs of the course rather than in the protest room.

However, when you are fouled and you believe that you are right according to the rules, you should protest—and you should take every precaution to make sure that your protest is upheld. Even before a foul, when you see a situation developing, you can help your chances later on by stating loudly and firmly what your rights are. You shouldn't be obnoxious or try to intimidate anyone, but such non-mandatory hails could conceivably strengthen your case at a protest hearing. Also, it draws the attention of nearby sailors who might act as witnesses in your behalf.

If you are fouled, you should quickly note the circumstances and the pertinent facts: your course and speed and those of the other party, the point of contact, the timing involved and possible witnesses. Once you have done this, immediately put these facts in the back of your mind until after the finish; the first priority is to get back to the business of racing. As long as you make these few important mental notes, you should easily be able to recall the complete incident once you get ashore. Trying to plan your protest strategy while still on the racecourse will only prevent you from concentrating on sailing.

Planning Your Protest

Once ashore, go directly to your rulebook. Even if the situation was relatively straightforward, you should read every rule that might conceivably relate. Find the rule or rules that specifically describe the incident. If you can't find the exact application in the rulebook, then go to the book of appeals— very rarely will you encounter a set of circumstances that are not specifically covered in the rules or the appeals. One of the most common reasons people lose protests when they are actually in the right is because they enter a protest meeting armed only with an intuitive sense of why they are right.

Put yourself in the other party's position. How is he likely to try to prove his case? Which of your facts might he possibly refute? What rules might serve his purpose? Say you are coming into the leeward mark on the starboard jibe, and in rounding have contact with an outside boat that approached on the port jibe. His only possible defenses are that you established your overlap too late, that you took too much room in rounding or that there was another boat that prevented him from keeping clear. You should be prepared to counter these attempts with facts and rules that refute his argument.

It is also useful to put yourself in the protest committee's place. In making a ruling on an incident, what facts are they likely to be looking for? What rules might they possibly consider? In a particularly sticky protest, what might be the key points that would clear up any direct disagreement between the protesting parties? For instance, you claim that you had to alter course for a boat that tacked below you at a weather mark, and the other boat is claiming that not only had he completed his tack, but also that you altered course down on him in the middle of his tack. To decide this protest, the committee will be interested in where you were at the time he began his tack, exactly when you began to alter course to keep clear, what your relative positions were immediately after the foul and what

the point of contact would have been had you held your course.

Rather than waiting to be questioned about the pertinent facts, you should put everything on the protest form. Think carefully about what you want to say before you begin writing. Then put down a clear, complete, to-the-point description of the incident. Print as neatly and legibly as possible—most committee members won't struggle very long over a sloppy protest form that is difficult to read. Put everything in chronological order; don't add additional facts onto the end.

Whenever possible, word your description using the phrasing of the rule under which you are protesting. For example: "Thirty seconds before the start, I established an overlap on a parallel course one boat length to leeward of US6377, who was slowly reaching down the line on starboard. *Providing ample room and opportunity to keep clear,* I hailed, "I'm coming up,' and then began to *carry out my luff slowly.* US6377 first did not respond and then only slowly. After four or five seconds had passed, I hailed again. Then, after another four or five seconds, *before reaching a closehauled course,* my starboard side, two feet in front of the shroud, made contact with the windward boat directly abeam of his traveler." This description immediately tells the protest committee that you have complied with all the requirements of a leeward boat luffing before the start, as prescribed in Rule 40.

Take equal care and pains in drawing your diagram of the incident. Make a trial sketch before putting it on your protest form, making sure that all angles and distances are accurate to the best of your knowledge. Don't forget that the jury will be trying to gain some insight into the facts through your drawing. If your boats are

169

The Right to Appeal

A sailor who feels that he has been mistakenly disqualified through a misapplication or misinterpretation of the rules by a jury has the right to appeal his protest to a higher committee. However, an appeal to a decision will be heard only if there is a direct question on the rules. Questions on the facts in a case are not grounds for appeal. A protest committee's determination of the facts are final.

The protest committee must grant permission for an appeal. If they do so, and they normally do, the facts go to a district appeals committee. Only the words of the protest committee are accepted by the appeals committee. Since only an interpretation of the rules is being asked for, no new testimony is heard. From the existing facts, the committee either upholds or reverses the original decision.

Appealing a decision can be a lengthy process. In fact, either party involved in a protest can appeal a district committee decision by taking the case to the national appeals committee. In the end, regardless of who was right or wrong, the rules are refined and clarified when the decision is released to the racing public. Eventually, appeals cases can form the basis for a change in the racing rules themselves.

---

drawn in different sizes or it is difficult to tell which way they are pointed or the distances and positions are inaccurate, the committee will be misled, possibly to your detriment. Draw a line through the bow and stern of your boats to show their exact headings. You might also find it to your advantage to identify the number of boat lengths to a mark or the number of feet separating boats. When drawing a sequence of positions, identify the time separating each stage of the action.

Fill in all of the blanks on the protest form as accurately as possible, even if you think that the information asked for is irrelevant. Include the exact rule numbers under which you are protesting. If it is a relatively straightforward protest, simply state the one rule that covers the situation; don't cloud the issue with a lot of other rules that don't directly apply. On the other hand, if it is a complex situation and you are not

sure what rule you should protest under, list all rules and appeals that appear to be applicable.

If you have a witness, spend some time talking to him before the hearing. Obviously, it is not ethical to coach a witness on what to say—in fact, this can backfire if the committee's questioning goes beyond your coaching. What you should do is simply listen to the witness's account of the incident, ask him the questions that the jury or the other party might ask, and then decide whether he will help or hurt you in a hearing. Sometimes a witness who means well simply does not have a clear picture of the situation. (Don't forget that a witness is at a disadvantage in that he may not be present for any of the other testimony.) Either because of his point of view or because he was, after all, a disinterested party, a witness's story might not match your own in certain details. In such cases, you are better off letting your account stand on its own rather than taking a chance that the jury might be misled by an unclear or partially contradictory account of the incident.

Conduct at the Protest Hearing

When entering a protest hearing, you should know your rights under Part VI and Appendix 6 of the USYRU Rules. Basically, these state that you are entitled to be present during the hearing, that you have a right to hear any and all testimony, that you may call witnesses, that you may question the other party or any witnesses, and that you are entitled to a written decision and an explanation of it.

In addition to your rights in a hearing, you also have several responsibilities. First of all, you should respect both the jury and the other party. Protest hearings and jury decisions are the fairest and most efficient means of deciding disagreements in what is still a gentleman's sport. All involved should act accordingly. Do not speak unless you are spoken to, even though the other skipper may present facts which do not seem accurate to you. It is important to listen quietly until it is your turn to speak. When your turn comes, look directly at the committee and talk *to* them, not *at* them. Do not look down at them or turn away. Respect them as the jury and speak in a positive tone. Be cordial and firm. Do not speak in anger and never use foul language.

When presenting your case, it is important to establish the facts as you remember them and to say exactly what happened. If you are uncertain on a point when questioned, then state that you are not sure. This is much better than trying to hedge and come up with some sort of vague answer. Speak in precise terms. For example: "At two to three boat lengths before the

mark, we were half a boat length apart," or "The collision occurred 10 seconds before the start." Do not say: "I think there were several boat lengths between us," or "It was about the time the starting gun went off . . ." As with your written testimony, try to state the facts in the context of the rules.

During your testimony, be brief and concise. Don't belabor a single point, although a good technique is to go back to key points when questioned or when questioning a witness. This is a delicate area. An experienced protest committee that knows the rules does not like to be told what is important and what is not, and definitely does not like to be told how to interpret the facts. Be careful not to be too obvious in bringing attention to what you feel are the key points. On the other hand, if the jury is not an experienced one and is possibly not quite as familiar with the rules as you are, don't hesitate to tactfully point out rules or appeals or facts important to your case that they seem to be overlooking. Before the hearing, try to find out who the jury members are and how experienced they are. During the hearing, try to estimate their grasp of the rules and the situation. The quality and personality of the jury will, to an extent, determine how you present your case.

One further piece of advice—once you have given your testimony, do not change your story. The single factor that seems to hurt sailors most in protests is changing testimony halfway through the hearing. Bringing up new information or facts that change what has already been said merely makes a jury believe that you are not certain of the facts. This is an important point to remember. A protest committee reaches a decision by relating the facts of an incident to what is prescribed by the racing rules.

If you cannot get your facts across to the jury, either because of unclear testimony or a lack of credibility, your chances of winning the protest are severely handicapped.

Carefully plan your protest, present the facts, both written and verbally, in a clear, organized manner and, unless you feel there are valid grounds for an appeal, ac-cept the jury's decision. And finally, possibly the most important step in a protest, whether you win or lose, is to learn from the experience. In fact, you will probably find, as I have, that the rules you know best are the ones under which you've been dis-qualified at one time or another.

Notes on Exercises, Clothing, Nutrition, and Mental Preparation

Whenever you go sailing, the first thing to do is stretch your muscles. On cold, windy days you will need more time to stretch to get your body into shape. Stretch slowly and smoothly, putting consistent tension on the muscles instead of jerking them. Try to do exercises that give you a full range of motion, as well as ones that prepare you for what you will be doing on the boat—trimming sheets, grinding winches, handling the wheel, hiking, whatever. It is also important to do stretching *after* a day's sailing, so that your muscles do not stiffen overnight.

To be able to sail well, you must be dressed appropriately. People simply do not function well when they are wet, cold, or overheated. If you are going on a long-distance race, find out the weather patterns you are likely to encounter. Read the magazine accounts of past races, or talk to people who have done the race before. And of course, listen to the National Weather Service forecast. Make it a rule to take a little more clothing than you need—better safe than sorry.

Many people do not like to pay for good foul-weather gear, but once on an ocean race they'd give anything for it. There are two basic kinds of foul-weather gear: light for warm weather, heavy for cold. Chest-high pants are best, because they do not easily take in water. Crisscross the straps in both the front and back, so that they do not fall off your shoulders. Pick a foul-weather jacket with a good hood and a front that permits no rain to trickle in. The best boots are nonskid—the higher the better. Wool sweaters are good because they resist water and also stay warm even when wet. Chambray shirts are comfortable and warm. Since much of your body heat escapes through your head, a wool hat is es-

sential in cold weather. In warm weather, a pair of gym shorts is perfect.

Sunglasses are a must in both cold and warm weather if the sun is out. Like any other part of your body, eyes can get sunburned, and they take two to three weeks to heal when they do. Also to prevent sunburn, keep a shirt on for a good part of the day. A hat, too. If you get hot, wet your hand with cold water and touch the back of your neck; it will quickly cool you. Sailing barefoot is not a good idea, because it is easy to cut your feet. Shoes make you more mobile as well as better protected, and wearing socks with shoes causes less slippage.

In dinghy sailing, one-piece jumpsuits are becoming popular because they keep you warm and dry. For good, secure hiking, choose boots that lace firmly around your ankle. Sailing gloves can be helpful, and once again, it is important to wear a hat. For protection against the sun, keep a small kit on board with sun-screening lotion, zinc oxide, and a suntanning lotion. When in doubt about your swimming ability, wear a life jacket. There are a number of styles that are very comfortable, warm and Coast Guard–approved.

To sail well you must eat well. The night before a regatta, eat normally, excluding exotic foods. Do not take any alcohol and do not eat acidic (gas-producing) or greasy foods. You may consider eating extra carbohydrates to store energy: potatoes, pasta, bread. But don't stuff yourself the night before a special event.

On the morning of the race, try to eat breakfast about two and a half to three hours before sailing. The timing of the meal can be as important as what you eat. Your energy during the race will come from the food you ate the night before anyway, so there is no need for a big breakfast, though it is useful for killing hunger pangs during the day. If you are tense, eat lightly. Otherwise, a normal breakfast is sufficient (but stay away from pork or fat).

Between races during the day or during a race, it is essential to drink liquids—Gatorade, ice water, iced tea for the summer; hot soup in cold weather. Swallowing liquids helps to clear your thinking. Even in single-handed boats you should be able to manage a few sips during a race, from a container brought along for the purpose. Stay away from carbonated drinks; they produce gas.

Foods high in glucose—candy bars and sugared gum, for example—produce short bursts of energy, but in the long run sap your energy by causing the blood to shift from the stomach to the muscles. With no energy left in the stomach, you become fatigued.

In a study done at a collegiate regatta, the Timme Angsten Memorial Regatta, held by the Chicago Yacht Club each year, it was found that the bottom five finishers did not feel that mental preparation was important at all and had not tried to prepare themselves mentally before the race. Obviously, they had made a mistake.

Certainly, every sailor should feel himself getting psyched up before a regatta. The problem is that many people get nervous, and this can interfere with their performance. A good way to combat nervousness the night before a race is to visualize yourself, as clearly and in as much detail as possible, doing everything you will be doing the next day in the race. Picture yourself walking down to the boat, getting into the boat, rigging the sails, sailing out to the starting line, checking which end is favored, maneuvering for the start, rounding marks, setting spinnakers, and so on. The more orderly and precise your visualization, the better. This is the "déjà vu" technique that seems to work so well for many athletes. Skiers, for example, will close their eyes and picture themselves racing down the slalom course, so when they actually make their run they are better prepared and, consequently, more relaxed, having been "down once" already. It works in sailing too.

If you find that once the race gets under way you are not doing well, get back to basics. Sail strictly by the numbers, going through each operation methodically.

In offshore racing, remember that being psyched up is good only while it lasts, and you must not expend all your mental and physical energies at the beginning. Inexperienced sailors in offshore races tend to do just that, working very hard and doing well in the early part of the race, only to fade later because they have not paced themselves. You have to adopt a comfortable routine early, standing your normal watches, so that you can be just as aggressive and tough at the finish as you are at the start.

Finally, a word about longer-range mental preparation. Many sailors never improve because they don't build on the past or plan for the future. To avoid this, first of all keep a logbook, in which you jot down things you learn from any source. It's important to know what you know. Then set goals for yourself: goals for the summer—the club championship, the national championship, being able to handle a boat, for example—and for the next few years. Then go out and work to achieve them. Whether or not you succeed, you will have made a lot more progress than you would have had you not had any goal in mind.

Glossary

abandonment   race that the race committee declares void at any time after the starting signal. The race can be resailed at the committee's discretion.

abeam   at right angles to the centerline of a boat

aft(er)   toward the stern of a boat

afterguard   members of crew stationed near the stern. They are responsible for making the major decisions. On a twelve-meter the afterguard consists of a skipper (usually the helmsman), a tactician, and a navigator.

(sailing) **against the grain**   approaching a fleet of boats, normally on a starting line, from the opposite direction

(sailing by) **air speed**   measuring the boat's speed using apparent wind as a benchmark, because a boat's instruments are more sensitive to a change in wind than to a change in the hull's speed through the water.

America's Cup   sailboat racing's most prestigious trophy. It is awarded to the winner of a match-race series between twelve-meter boats (best of seven races), held every three to four years in Newport, Rhode Island.

amidships   between fore and aft; the middle of a boat

anemometer   instrument used to measure apparent wind velocity

angle of heel   the angle at which a boat is leaning

apparent wind   the wind felt over the deck of a boat: the true wind plus the wind created by the boat's movement

appeals   additions to the racing rules used to interpret situations that are not specifically covered in the racing rules

(sailing) **around the world**   being caught in a continuous lift so that the boat stays far from a mark during a rounding, making for an unnecessarily longer course

aspect ratio   the ratio between the height and width of the rig

astern   behind the stern of a boat

athwartships   across the beam of a boat, outboard or inboard

baby stay   a wire used to bend the mast forward, normally attached to the deck halfway between the bow and mast

back   to trim a sail, usually the jib, to the windward side, causing the boat to spin on its new course faster

backing wind   a wind shift in a counterclockwise direction

backstay   a wire support from the mast to the stern of the boat

backwind   a backlash of wind, from the jib to the main or from a leeward boat to a windward boat

bag   to increase the draft of a sail by easing off all adjustments; to make a sail fuller

balanced boat   a boat tuned so that all weights and forces are evenly distributed. The boat will therefore sail a straight course by itself, without the tiller's being held: there is no "helm."

barber hauler   an extra line used to change the sheeting angle of a jib or spinnaker. Normally used in flat water to get the boat to point higher.

barging   approaching a fleet of boats to leeward on a course below close-hauled

batten   one of two or three wooden or fiber-glass shafts that fit into pockets on the leech of a sail. They control its shape by preventing the leech from sagging toward the mast.

beam   the width of a boat at its widest

beam reach   *see* "reaching"

bear off   to change course away from the wind

beat   to sail to windward

bias   a line running diagonally, across the vertical and horizontal threads, on a sailcloth. A sail will be pulled out of shape if stretched along the bias.

Biss mark   mark drawn on the middle of the boom, pointing toward the head of the sail. Helps locate draft position.

(taking a) **bite**   altering course toward the wind to gain windward distance

blanketing zone   the area of bad wind caused by one boat to windward of another boat, obstructing its wind

blocker   a boat that sails across the fleet giving one clear air by forcing other boats off one's wind

blooper   a staysail made of spinnaker cloth. Set to leeward of a spinnaker when the wind is aft of 135 degrees.

boat speed   the speed of a boat, particularly its potential speed in comparison with that of other boats

boomvang   a mechanical apparatus used to tighten the leech of the mainsail. Can be a block and tackle rig or a hydraulic rod.

bow   forward part of the boat

bowman   crew member assigned to the forward part of the boat. He sets the spinnaker, calls the starting line, and normally is in charge of the foredeck crew.

breakdown   a broken piece of equipment handicapping a boat

breaking through   sailing through the blanketing zone of another boat

broach   to spin out of control and capsize or come close to it; loss of steering

broad reach   point of sail when the wind is slightly aft of abeam

bullet   first-place finish

buoy room   the maneuvering space outside boats must give an inside boat at a mark (Rule 42)

(sailing) **by-the-lee**   sailing with the wind coming over the quarter of the boat where the main boom is set, thus pushing the boat to leeward rather than ahead; an occasional alternative to jibing, but an unsteady course in heavy winds

camber   *see* "draft"

campaign to sail in a series of regattas, usually culminating in a particularly important regatta

carbon fiber strong material used to stiffen parts of a boat: hull, centerboard, rudder, mast, boom, battens, etc.

cavitation instability that results from air being sucked between the centerboard, keel, or rudder and the hull. Often caused by too great an angle of heel.

centerboard shaped blade attached to the underside of the hull to give the boat lateral resistance when it is sailing to windward; an adjustable keel

centerline an imaginary line drawn from bow to stern, dividing the boat in half lengthwise

choke to overtrim sails so the wind stalls out, slowing the boat

chute slang for spinnaker

circuit a series of races over a period of time, whose results are combined to give an overall winner

Class A boats the largest boats in a fleet

clear air unobstructed wind

clear astern/ahead no overlap with a boat behind/ahead

cleat a fitting used to secure a line under strain

clew the outer corner of a sail along the boom. A spinnaker is sheeted at the clew.

clinometer an instrument, in the form of a semicircular level, indicating angle of heel and fore-and-aft trim

close-hauled most windward point of sail, at which the wind is well forward of abeam (90 degrees). Most boats can sail within 45 degrees to the wind. Twelve-meters can sail 35 degrees to the wind; the giant J's were able to sail about 28 degrees to the wind.

close reach point of sailing at which the wind is slightly forward of abeam

cockpit opening in the after section of boat where steering device is

coffee grinder winch used for trimming large sails. Separate handles are turned by a person called a "grinder." Twelve-meters use four grinders during a tack.

cone area between the two lay lines to a mark

cover to position your boat between your competition and the wind, not allowing the competition clear air

crabbing taking bites to windward before the starting line to capture the wind of an opponent

crack sheets to ease sheets when bearing off

cunningham a line that runs through an opening at the edge of the mainsail and controls its draft on the luff below the tack

current sheer the line along which two different currents meet. A current sheer is often marked by turbulent water, flotsam, and jetsam.

current stick floating device consisting of a weight attached to a stick that rises slightly above the waterline. The direction in which the stick moves and the angle at which it slants indicate the direction and strength of the current. Current sticks are found next to anchored objects, which serve as reference points.

custom boat   a boat built by a custom designer and builder. It is usually the only one of its kind.

deck sweeper   headsail with a low foot, which lies across the foredeck to trap air that otherwise might escape between the foot of the sail and the deck

dip   to bear away behind an approaching boat

dip start   a starting technique whereby one sits above the line, then reaches to get below it and heads up just before the starting gun is sounded

D. L.   a dead-last finish

downhaul   line attached to the tack of the sail; used to trim the draft forward

downwind   away from where the wind is coming

draft   1. the depth or fullness in a sail

 2. the depth of the keel or centerboard in the water

draft control   sail panel, usually triangular, that creates draft in a sail. This panel is usually one or two panels above the foot.

drafting   *see* "towing"

drive (also "dive")   to head off slightly, when sailing to windward, to gain extra speed

dual leads   a double set of sheets, usually on a genoa

duel   *see* "tacking duel"

ebb   outgoing tide

eddy   confused water current or disturbed wind

fair   1. smooth

 2. for the wind to move aft

fairlead   a fitting used to change the direction of a line, giving it a better angle from a sail or block to a winch or cleat

false tack   a tack that is begun only to be abandoned, in an attempt to trick the competition

favored   the better end of a starting line or course

feather   to head up into the wind in order to reduce the angle of heel or to take bites to windward

fetch a mark   to reach a mark with no change in course

finishing   A yacht finishes when any part of her hull, crew, or equipment crosses the finish line, coming from the direction of the last mark, after fulfilling her penalty obligations, if any, under Rule 52.2.

fire drill   the great activity (and usually confusion) when all crew members are scrambling to solve a sudden problem

fittings   equipment on the boat for securing lines and gear

flake sails   to fold sails

flanker   flat spinnaker used for reaching when the apparent wind is between 60 and 90 degrees

flat   on an even keel; no angle of heel

fleet racing   racing with more than two boats

floater takedown   dowsing a spinnaker by taking the pole down early. Normally done when a boat must jibe around a leeward mark.

foot   1. to head away from the wind to gain speed
  2. bottom part of a sail

forward (fore)   toward the bow of the boat

foxhole   section of a boat where all halyards, vangs, cunninghams, topping lifts, and miscellaneous lines are trimmed

front   the edge of a low-pressure system approaching an area, normally bringing rain and a change in wind and temperature

gaff   a pole extending from a mast to support the head of a sail

gaining bearing   advancing on or pulling away from another boat, as determined by sightings with a compass

general recall   the summoning of an entire fleet to return to the starting line for another start

genoa   an overlapping headsail

geographic shift   a wind shift caused by the local geography

getaway   popping out ahead of the fleet with clear air

grand prix racer   a boat designed and outfitted strictly for racing

grinding   turning the handles of winches to trim sails

guy   line or wire used to trim the spinnaker pole

halyard   line used to haul sails up and down the mast

hand-bearing compass   a small compass held by hand as one sights one's position (takes bearings) in regard to fixed points and/or other boats

handicap   a predesignated time advantage in a race, most commonly used to permit boats of different sizes to race against one another

harden up   to trim sails in order to sail closer to the wind

hard-a-lee   the command to inform the crew to be prepared for a tack—that the helm is being pushed hard to leeward, turning the boat into the wind

head   the top of a sail

header   a wind shift that forces a boat to bear off

headsail   any sail used forward of the mast, secured to the bow

headstay   a forward shroud supporting the mast

headstay sag   sag in the headstay caused by the force of wind in a sail

head off   *see* "bear off"

head up   to alter course toward the wind; to luff

heavy air   high wind

heel   to tilt to leeward

helm   1. the area of the stern where the boat is steered
2. the combination of forces on the rudder that causes the boat to round into or away from the wind. Windward helm rounds the boat into the wind, leeward helm away from the wind.

helmsman   person who steers the boat

(pointing) **high**   sailing close to the wind

hiking   leaning over the side of a boat to help counterbalance heeling

hiking stick   an extension of the tiller, allowing the helmsman to hike and still control the helm

hiking straps   footholds attached to the side of the boat, allowing the crew members to secure themselves while hiking

hole   an area of the water with less wind than the surrounding area

hull speed   the maximum attainable speed of a boat without planing or surfing

hydraulic ram   device for moving the mast

ICYRA   Intercollegiate Yacht Racing Association of North America

inboard   toward the centerline of the boat

inhaul   line used to pull the foot of the mainsail or a headsail forward

IOR   International Offshore Rule: the formula by which yachts are rated, according to their physical characteristics. A number in feet is arrived at, and this figure is applied to the length of the race to determine a boat's time handicap.

IYRU   International Yacht Racing Union: world governing body of yacht racing

jam cleat   device that secures a line with strong jaws through which the line is passed

jib   triangular sail set forward of the mainmast

jibe   A yacht begins to jibe at the moment when, with the wind aft, the foot of her mainsail crosses her centerline. The yacht completes the jibe when the mainsail has filled on the new tack.

jib lead   fairlead from where the jib clew position is set

jib man   crew member who trims the jib

jibsheet   line that trims the jib

jibstay   wire supporting the mast to which the luff of the jib is attached

jibstay sag   the sag in the jibstay caused by the force of the wind in the jib

J locks   shackles with a quick release, used for attaching the sheets to the clew of the jib

J measurement   the distance between the mast and the headstay

keel   a heavy fin under the hull. The keel prevents a boat from sideslipping by resisting the sideways force of the wind.

keelboat   a boat with a keel

kicker (kicking strap)   *see* "boomvang"

knockdown   sudden and extreme heeling due to a strong gust of wind

lateral resistance   force of the keel or centerboard counteracting the sideways force on the sails by the wind

lay line   the best line a boat can sail to fetch a mark

lead   *see* "fairlead"

lead boat   *see* "blocker"

leech   the after edge of a sail. A "tight" leech on a mainsail forms almost a perpendicular with the deck. A "loose" leech forms a curved line.

leeward   away from the wind

leeward helm   *see* "helm"

(make) leeway   to move sideways through the water; sideslip

leg   the course between two buoys; a part of the racing course

level racing   racing between boats of different designs but of the same handicap

lift   a change in the direction of the wind allowing a boat to sail closer to the desired course when sailing upwind, away from it when sailing downward

light air   winds of low velocity

line squall   a sudden storm, with high winds and heavy rain

low   directed away from the wind (as in "a low course")

luff   1. the forward vertical edge of a sail

2. to alter course toward the wind until the boat is head to wind

3. the flapping of a sail caused by the boat being head to wind

luffing rights   a yacht's option to hurt an opponent's air by luffing when by the rules it is in a privileged position

luff round   the curve of the forward edge of a sail. This shape creates draft when the luff is attached to the mast, which is straight.

mainsail   the after sail attached to the mainmast

main trim   the position of the mainsail inboard or outboard

"making trees"   gaining distance on a competitor, gauged by an increasing (or, if one is behind, a decreasing) number of trees onshore that corresponds to the gap between the boats

mark   any object specified in the sailing instructions as one that a yacht must round or pass on a required side. Every ordinary part of a mark is considered part of it, including a flag, flagpole, boom, or anchored boat, but excluding ground tackle and any object either accidentally or temporarily attached to the mark.

mark rounding   the turn around a mark during a race

mast abeam   the hail to another boat when it no longer has luffing rights—*i.e.,* when the helmsman sighting abeam is in line with the mainmast of the leeward yacht. (Note: the two boats must be on a parallel course, and the helmsman must make the hail.)

masthead   the top of a mast

masthead fly   a small flag on the top of a mast; indicates wind direction

mast partner   the strong setting that secures the mast at the deck

mast rake   the tilt fore or aft (if any) of the mast

mast ram   *see* "hydraulic ram"

match racing   a race of just two boats

MORC   Midget Ocean Racing Club, for boats between 20 and 30 feet long

navigator   crew member assigned to keep track of the boat's position, to determine apparent wind on the next leg, and to work with the skipper on strategy

obstruction   any object, including a vessel under way, large enough to require a yacht not less than one overall length away from it to make a substantial alteration of course to pass on one side or the other; any object that can be passed on one side only, including a buoy when the yacht in question cannot safely pass between it and the shoal or object it marks

Olympic scoring   system of scoring used by the IYRU for the Olympic Games and major regattas. It puts a premium on placing first, by heavily penalizing runners-up: first: 0; second: 3; third: 5.7; fourth: 8; fifth: 10; sixth: 11.7; and thereafter the number of the finish plus 6 (seventh: 13, eighth: 14, etc).

one-design boats   boats of exactly the same design (and potentially the same speed)

one-tonner   level-racing offshore yacht with an IOR rating of 27.5 feet

ooching   repetitive motion by the crew—shifting weight forward and stopping suddenly to move the boat forward

ORCA   Ocean Racing Club of America. This club promotes ocean racing in the United States

oscillating wind shift   a continual, back-and-forth change in the direction of the wind

outboard   away from the centerline of the boat

outhaul   line that pulls the mainsail away from the mast and tightens the foot of the sail along the boom

overlap   the situation when two boats are sailing on parallel courses within two overall lengths of each other and part of one boat lies forward of a line projecting abeam from the other's aftermost point

overpowered   too much sail up, or too much draft in the sail, forcing the boat to sail at too great an angle of heel

overstand   to sail past the lay line to a mark

overtrimmed   sails too tightly adjusted, with less draft (and therefore less power) than desired

passing lane   corridor to windward of a fleet of boats sailing on a leeward leg of a course; the route one normally takes to pass

phasing   tacking in conjunction with wind shifts

PHRF   Performance Handicap Racing Formula. This formula determines a racing handicap on the basis of past performances.

pinch   to sail too high for the sails to work at their optimal level

pitching moment   the fore-and-aft motion of a boat

planing   riding on the water rather than through it; characteristic of light, high-performance boats

pointing   sailing close to the wind

points of sailing   the different angles a boat can make with the wind. There are three general types: beating (wind forward of a beam), reaching (wind abeam), and running (wind aft of a beam).

port   the left side of a boat as one faces forward

port approach   *see* "against the grain"

prejibe   a jibe begun by pushing the mainsail across the boat early, before the wind has crossed the centerline. This helps the boat turn faster. Used in match-race starts.

proper course   course a yacht would sail in the absence of other yachts. Used in certain situations as a standard for judging whether or not a course alteration to slow down an opponent was permissible. There is no proper course before the starting signal.

protest   an alleged violation of the rules on the racecourse, prompting a hearing by a committee of judges to decide if the violation has in fact occurred. A protest can be initiated by any competitor, the race committee, or the jury.

puff   an increase in wind velocity across the water

pumping   the rapid trimming of sails for speed

racing   a yacht is racing from the preparatory signal until she has finished and cleared the finishing line and finishing marks.

rating   the figure, arrived at by formula, on which a boat's handicap is based

reacher   full jib used when sailing a reaching course

reversal   a change of positions whereby the tactical advantage passes from one boat to the other

rhumb line   the straight-line compass course between two points, particularly two marks

rig   a boat's sails, mast, and rigging

righting moment   the natural movement of a boat toward an upright position

roach   the area of the sail between the middle of the head, the clew, and the leech

rocking   shifting weight to move a boat to leeward and back to windward in order to help create wind in the sails

roll jibe   a jibe assisted by a rolling of the boat by the crew. As the boat rolls, wind is created in its sails, so less course change is required.

roll tack   a tack assisted by a rolling of the boat by the crew, again to increase acceleration and lessen the required course change

run   point of sailing when the wind is aft

sag   *see* "headstay sag"

sailmaker   person who designs, builds, and repairs sails

sail trim   the position of the sails

scull   to move the rudder rapidly back and forth to propel the boat forward

sea breeze   wind created when the land heats up, the warm air above it rises, and the cooler air over the sea moves to fill in

series   a set number of races

sewer man   crew member on a twelve-meter who works belowdecks, handling halyards and packing sails

sheeting   the line or lines that control a given spar or sail

shifting gears   adjusting sail trim and balance of the boat as the wind and sea conditions change

shooting the line (mark)   heading up just before crossing the finish line (or rounding a mark) to decrease the distance between the boat and the line (or mark), so that the boat reaches it sooner

shrouds   vertical wires that hold the mast upright

sideslip   *see* "leeway"

sidestays   shrouds extending from the boat sides that help to hold up the mast

sight   to take a bearing on an object with a hand-bearing compass or a sextant

S-jibe   a controlled jibe, designed to reduce the force of wind on a sail during the jibe in order to prevent the boat from becoming unstable

skipper   the person in command of the boat, usually the helmsman

slot   the gap between the mainsail and headsail or spinnaker

SORC   Southern Ocean Racing Circuit: series of ocean races around Florida in February each year

spar   mast, boom, or gaff

speed stripes   horizontal stripes (usually two or three) on a sail used to help one determine draft position

speed testing   practice technique by which two boats run through sailing trials together to determine relative speeds

spinnaker   balloonlike sail used on leeward legs. It is set from the mast and a boom extending from the mast (spinnaker pole).

split   to sail away from the competition

spreaders   supports that keep the shrouds away from the mast, for better mast-bend control

stack   a cluster of slowly moving boats all on the same tack

starboard   the right side of a boat as one faces forward

starting   A yacht starts when, after the starting signal, any part of her hull, crew, or equipment crosses the starting line in the direction of the course to the first mark

stay   *see* "shroud"

staysail   small triangular sail used forward of the mast on reaching legs

stern   the after section of the boat

stick   the mast

surfing   riding waves to increase speed

syndicate   group of backers of a sailing campaign

tack   1. the forward lower area of a sail, where the luff and foot meet

2. point of sailing when the boat is heading to windward

3. to change course by passing into the wind. A yacht is tacking from the time she is beyond head-to-wind until she has assumed a close-hauled course, if sailing to windward. If she is not sailing to windward, the tack is completed when her mainsail fills on the new course

tacking duel   two boats maneuvering against each other on a windward leg of a race by tacking back and forth

tacking lines   sighting lines drawn on the deck, used to determine the boat's position in relation to other boats and also to marks. This information is often essential in deciding when to tack.

tactician   crew member who informs the skipper of the boat's position in the race and recommends tactics to improve it

tactics   the maneuvering decisions a boat makes in dealing with the wind, waves, and competition during a race

tailer   crew member in charge of trimming headsails and the spinnaker

telltales   light strings, usually made of yarn, attached to the sails and shrouds so as to stream in the wind and thereby indicate its direction

tiller   steering instrument that controls the rudder

timed run   a starting technique whereby a boat runs away from the line for a predetermined time, then returns so as to hit the starting line with speed at the starting signal

topping lift   line from the mast to the spinnaker pole, controlling pole height and the draft position of the spinnaker—pole down: draft forward; pole up: draft aft

towing   sailing behind a bigger boat to gain speed from its following waves

trapeze   a wire that hangs from the mast and when attached to a harness permits a crew member to stand out on the windward rail. Normally used on high-performance boats.

traveler a sliding fitting to which the mainsheet is attached, keeping the boom in the same plane as it is moved in and out

triangular start starting technique by which a boat sails a short triangular course in order to achieve momentum and a good position on the starting line at the start

trim to adjust sails

trim tab rudder at the after edge of the keel when there is a split rudder (*i.e.*, two rudders). Can be used independently of or in conjunction with the other rudder.

true wind the speed and direction of the wind on its own, not including the wind generated by the moving boat

tune up to adjust the rigging for balance and speed. Often achieved through speed testing

twelve meters the waterline length of yachts used for the America's Cup competition since 1958

undertrimmed sails that are eased too much

upwind to windward

USISA United States International Sailing Association: organization for promoting international competition

USYRU United States Yacht Racing Union: the American governing authority of yachting

vang *see* "boomvang"

vang sheeting sheeting that can be used with a boomvang, to eliminate the need for a traveler—keeping the boom in the same plane as it is moved in and out

wake waves from a boat

winch mechanical device to aid in pulling a line. It consists basically of a coil, on which the line is wound, and a crank, to do the winding.

windage turbulence caused by objects protruding into the wind

windshadow *see* "blanketing zone"

wind sheer the phenomenon of wind at the top of the sail flowing in a different direction from wind at the bottom

wind shift change in the direction of the wind

windward toward the wind; opposite of leeward

windward helm *see* "helm"

winged out sail position with the mainsail on one side of the boat and the jib on the other; used on a run with the wind aft of 135 degrees

yawing drifting off course and having difficulty steering

Index

National Weather Service, 98, 174

Offshore racing, 14, 21, 35, 46; handicap vs. one-design, 35. *See also* specific races; specific sailboats.
Olympics, 14, 20, 112; Commette, Peter, in, 112; trials (1976), 112; and local wind sources, 99–100; Turner, Ted, winning in the, 20
One-design sailing, 35
One-tonners, 87
Oscillating shift, 97
Overshooting the mark, 125
Overstanding a windward mark, 131, 133

Penguin, 17, 20
Persistent shift, 98
Pied Piper, 16
Planing, 84
Port approach, 108–10
Port tack: lead-boat blocker technique and, 119; start, 113
Practice, 22, 28, 89
Pre-jibe, 77
Prestart tune-up, 104–05; angle of waves and, 101; using the buddy system in, 104
Protecting the downwind position, 144
Protests, 168–70, 171-72; right to appeal and, 170; USYRU rules and rights in, 168
"Protests and Appeals," 167–72

Racecourse tactics and strategy, 97–149. *See also* After rounding the leeward mark; Coming off the line; Finish; Maneuvering; Prestart tune-up; Reading the elements; Rounding the reach mark and the leeward mark; Rounding the windward mark, sailing the leeward leg; Starting techniques; Windward tactics.
Reading the elements, 97–104. *See also* Current; Waves; Wind.
Reversal, 153, 154-55
Roll jibe, 77, 78
Roll tacking, 74
Rounding the leeward mark, 143, 145–46, 165
Rounding the reach mark and the leeward mark, 143, 145–47
Rounding the windward mark, 135–38, 141–42, 161–62
Rudder, 45, 66, 68, 80
Rule 41, 121
Rule 42.3A (I and II), 137.

See also Rounding the windward mark.
Rule 39, 138,141
Rule 37, 138
Running Tide, 22
Ryder, Stretch, 34

Sailboat racing, 13, 174, 175
Sailing: by air vs. boat speed, 142; clothing for, 174; food and drink for, 174–75; vocation vs. hobby, 40–41; in waves, 102; winning in, 125
Sailing by-the-lee, 16, 80–83, 86
Sailing into a header, 100
Sailing on a lift, 129, 143
"Sailing on its lines," 26, 50. *See also* Angle of heel; Balance.
Sailing the leeward leg, 136-43
Sailmaker, 21, 41, 45, 59. *See also* America's Cup.
Sail selection, 66, 104, 153
Sail trim, 73, 80, 93, 101; and prestart tune-up, 104; and rounding the mark, 136–37.
Sail trimmer, 59, 66, 93. *See also* specific sails.
Sea breeze, 99
Shields, 13, 108
Shooting the line, 149
S-jibe, 80
Small boats, 58, 83, 100–101
Small-boat sailers, "wear their boats," 66
Solings, 108
Southern Ocean Racing Conference (SORC) races, 16, 40
Speed. *See* Boat speed.
Speed stripes, 53
Speed testing, 90, 92; buddy system in, 104
Spinnaker, 50, 60–63, 64, 66, 77, 84–85; downwind sailing with, 147; and rounding the mark, 138. *See also* Maneuvering; specific techniques.
Spreaders, 45–46
Stack, 108, 114, 116, 131
Starboard-tack advantage, 110, 112, 125, 131, 134
Starting techniques, 105, 106–08, 110, 112–14, 116, 154; on *Courageous,* 107. *See also* specific techniques.
Staysail, 50, 63–64
Steering, 66–68, 70–71; in choppy conditions, 70–71; driving, 71; pinching, 71; and wave pattern, 101; to windward, 68

Acknowledgments

Many thanks to the United States Naval Academy for providing the boats and equipment for many of the pictures in section two, and to Pat Healy, Tim McGee, and Darrel Van Hutton for doing the demonstrations.

Thanks also to Michael Crowley for his help with meteorology, and to Fritz Hagerman for information on nutrition and stretching.

The section on protests and appeals is reprinted with the permission of Yacht Racing/Cruising Magazine.

Photo Credits

Christopher Cunningham: 4-5, 31 bottom, 41 bottom, 42-43
Bob Dollard: 2–3, 18–19, 58 both, 60–61, 67, 70 both, 74 both, 75 all four, 79 all four, 83, 84 top, 85 both, 86 both, 87 both, 114–15
Grant Donaldson: 15, 47 top
Daniel Forster: 10–11, 24–25, 26–27, 32–33, 56–57, 68–69, 73 left, 88, 89 bottom, 116–17, 149, 150–51, 156–57, 158, 159.
Shelley Heller: 94–95
Bob Johnstone (J Boats, Inc.): 36
Ray Medley: 89 top, 136, 139, 147
Betsey Rounersville: 31 top
Carol Singer: 23, 47 bottom, 63, 68, 73 right, 84 bottom, 163, 164
Marshall Winder: 17, 24, 29, 30, 55, 91
Windsurfer International: 36–37, 38–39